MW01678833

SEX, VICE & MORALITY

Tales from a Detective's Notebook

Robert M. Welsh

© Robert M. Welsh 1994

Welsh, Robert M.
Sex, Vice & Morality: Tales from a Detective's Notebook

ISBN 0-9698639-0-X
1. Sex crimes–British Columbia–Vancouver. 2. Vancouver (B.C.). Police Dept. 3. Welsh, Robert M. I. Title.
HV8079.S48W44 1994 363.2'5953'0971133 C94-910635-6

No part of this publication may be stored in a retreival system, transmitted or reproduced in any way, including but limited to photocopy, photograph, magnetic or other record, without the prior agreement and written approval of the author.

Editorial assistance, typesetting and design by Pat Meehan

Table of Contents

Prologue

Violent sex crimes are on the rise all over the world. Mass murderers are becoming more prevalent as days go by.

Can we, as police officers, do more to stem the growing tide of murders and rapes? How many police investigators have lain awake at night, exhausted from hours of overtime spent trying desperately to come up with a suspect? Unable to sleep now, haunted by the fear that he may be missing a clue, that a suspect already questioned and cleared is, in fact, guilty. And those 4 am phone calls. Another violent rape or murder following the same pattern, pointing to the same suspect. Could we have done more, why have we not arrested this animal? Another father and mother to face, their faces wrought with grief and frustration, their child mutilated in body and in spirit. What system can we possibly use to apprehend and convict sexual offenders who are often released by juries and judges, when they are as guilty as Hell? Did we miss some evidence along the way that might have sealed the offender's fate?

These problems are reported worldwide. In Switzerland, half the men convicted of rape never go to jail. In West Germany, less than one rape victim in ten makes a formal complaint to police. In Scotland, in 1980, a Glasgow prosecutor decided not to proceed with charges against three teenagers who raped a woman and slashed her thirty-eight times with a knife, giving as his reason that the victim was too ill to testify. The victim herself vigorously denied this. In response, Prime Minister Margaret Thatcher fired the Solicitor General for Scotland.

The case of the Yorkshire Ripper speaks for itself. Although he was questioned several times, it took British police five years to arrest and charge Peter Sutcliffe. It is reported that, early in the investigation, one Detective had submitted a report identifying Sutcliffe as the prime suspect. How many additional victims lost their lives since the report was submitted is not clear, but it certainly appears that more could have been done. On many occasions, large police forces have so many investigators involved that they lose track of the facts. The advent of computerized reporting and cross-referencing should alleviate most of these difficulties in the future.

Truth, or at least a scrap of information, often nothing more than innuendo to begin with, is always a valuable commodity, and must be paid for in one currency or another. Police officers have to deal with informants, better known as stool pigeons or snitches, throughout their entire careers. All the informants expect and usually get favours in the form of cash or the promise of lighter sentences or parole when they are eventually charged with some offence in return. This is just a different and probably necessary form of dealing with underworld scum.

These are the types of cases that many police forces all over the world are facing. The following cases are authentic; most were reconstructed from my official police files, as well as memory allows.

These stories are being re-told, not to remind victims of their anguish and loss, but as cautionary tales – a police presence will prevent certain kinds of crimes, and, after crimes have been committed, diligent police work will bring many criminals to justice – but a citizen's best protection is still a healthy degree of caution. Do not allow your family, your friends or yourself to be conned into becoming a victim.

The names of some of the persons described have been changed to preserve their privacy; many were borne along by events beyond their control and some went to pains to assist us in our duty. Any similarities between such aliases and the names of living persons is purely coincidental.

I dedicate this book to police officers everywhere.

The Players and the Ground

To clarify what might otherwise seem to be vague and confusing references in the book, this chapter offers a brief explanation of some of the jurisdictional relationships between the various municipal police forces and the RCMP, and describes the principal penal institutions in the province during the period covered by the events in this book.

Policing in British Columbia

The B.C. Provincial Police

Historically, organized policing in B.C. began in 1858, when James Douglas, governor of Vancouver Island, alarmed at the rush of 30,000 miners towards the Cariboo goldfields, petitioned for and received permission to raise a police force to ensure the maintenance of order. At Fort Langley, on November 19, 1858, when Douglas was sworn in as the first governor of the new Crown colony of British Columbia, the British Columbia Police also came into being. When B.C. joined Confederation in 1871, 'Provincial' was added.

It was a curious force, relying primarily on the reputation of its officers, the shine of its badges (uniforms were only issued in 1923), and that so fragile commodity, respect for the law, but it grew into one of the most progressive and respected police forces in North America. Radio-equipped cars, motorcycle-mounted highway patrols, police boats, airplanes, training programs and forensic techniques swelled its arsenal as its centennial drew nearer. It never got there.

The Provincial Police served British Columbia admirably until August 15, 1950, when its duties were assumed by the RCMP, which secretly and not-so-secretly, yearned to be a national police force. The RCMP Commissioner undoubtedly felt that eliminating the B.C. Police was an important step to achieving this goal. They have, however, failed in this aim, as Ontario and Quebec steadfastly maintain their own Provincial Police Forces.

The Royal Canadian Mounted Police

Founded on May 23, 1873, as the North-West Mounted Police (the 'Royal' was added in 1904), the force acquired its present name in 1920, when it absorbed its weak rival, the

Dominion Police. Prior to the appearance of the Mounties, policing in what was to become Manitoba, Saskatchewan, Alberta, the Northwest Territories, the Yukon and other remote northern communities was undertaken by the Hudson's Bay Company; this activity was understandably centred around its trading posts and it probably amounted to little more than maintaining a quiet atmosphere for trade.

Other provincial police forces, some created by expediency during the manpower shortages of WW I, also succumbed to the RCMP's national thirst: Manitoba (1870 - 1932), Saskatchewan (1917 - 1928) and Alberta (1917 - 1932). While the FBI under J. Edgar Hoover was more flamboyant, the same driving hunger for national police status was evident in Regina and was carefully handed down from Commissioner to Commissioner in the RCMP.

Debate on the original purpose of RCMP continues. Whether it was to protect the Indians from the unscrupulous exploitation of the whiskey traders, who were mostly but not entirely 'Boston Men,' (Americans) or whether it was meant to be a para-military force to keep order, white man style, while the government gained 'legal' control of the tribal lands is arguable. Along the way, Parliament gave it other duties and it invented even more tasks for itself.

The RCMP fields approximately 20,000 members across Canada; over 2,000 of these provide municipal policing in nearly 200 towns and municipalities, ranging in size from remote one-man detachments to its 270-plus Surrey force. Under its mandate to enforce the Explosives Act, the Narcotic Control Act, the Food and Drugs Act, the Indian Act and the Customs and Excise Acts, the force is found in cities which maintain their own police forces, such as Vancouver and Victoria and other ports of entry. Unless directed by the federal government, it does not normally enforce the provisions of the Criminal Code of Canada; such investigations arelikely to be into drug-related conspiracy charges or allegations of the fraudulent use of public funds.

The RCMP operates the Canadian Police Information Centre (CPIC) in Ottawa, a computerized information system which provides all other police forces in Canada with rapid access to current information on wanted or missing persons, stolen property, the status of warrants and stolen or abandoned car and boats. Under its 'L' Directorate, it operates the Crime Detection Laboratories and Identification Services, which provide specialized forensic assistance, fingerprint banks, criminal history files and so on.

On the eve of its centennial in 1973, the publication of *The Unauthorized History of the RCMP* created a furore. It alleged a long history of illegal activities. In addition, the Force has proven itself to be very thin-skinned; in the 60s or 70s, they sent a 'cease and desist' letter to the producers of the American cartoon show 'Rocky and Bullwinkle,' who regularly featured the inept Dudley Do-Right of the Mounties, and in the early 90s, tried the same thing over some TV ads in Britain which employed a Mountie character. It is not surprising, then, that Vancouver's National Basketball Association franchise will not call its team the Mounties. I certainly knew some who had a healthy sense of humour and could withstand a good laugh at themselves.

One of the unresolved difficulties of municipal policing by the RCMP is that, while responsible in a legal sense to the provincial Attorney-General, all the B.C. detachments are still subject to orders from Headquarters in Ottawa, from which flow technical directives and those all-important carrer moves and promotions..

Municipal Police Forces

Locally, the cities of Vancouver, New Westminster, Port Moody and the municipalities of West Vancouver and Delta all maintain their own police forces. Victoria, Saanich, Matsqui and some of the other larger communities field independent forces as well, but they do not figure in the stories that follow. These forces are responsible for enforcing all the laws of their local jurisdictions, including the provisions of the Criminal Code of Canada, provincial statutes and the bylaws of their respective municipalities. Recently, some federal statutes such as the Narcotic Control Act and The Food and Drugs Act have been delegated to them as well. With the advent of regional police services, these forces may eventually take over some territories and responsibilities from the RCMP.

On May 10, 1886, John Stewart became the first constable of the new City of Vancouver. He had previously been the Merchant's Patrolman, hired privately "...to prowl the streets after dark, see where the trouble lay and to do what he can to stop it." In the wake of the great fire of June 13, 1886, Stewart literally press-ganged the first man he found. When he and additional men were sworn in, American silver dollars, whose front faces had been ground clean and re-engraved with 'Vancouver City Police,' were made to serve as badges. Uniforms were bought in Seattle and with them came the American-style police helmets, with a more rounded crown and flatter brim than the English-style Bobby helmets that replaced them from 1907 to 1936.

1904 saw the Force move to Cordova and Main, where it is still located, although it has gone through three different buildings on that site.

Trouble, both external and internal, is the mainstay of police existence, and the Force saw its first corruption scandal in 1899; the Mounties of that era were suffering from insubordination and desertion – these are occasional problems that all forces must be prepared to deal with. Additional uproars occurred in 1928, 1934, 1948 and ended with the 1955 Tupper Royal Commission inquiry into graft and corruption. In each case, officers were dismissed and administrative and educational efforts were made to prevent recurrences.

1929 saw the Force's territory expand to its present size with the amalgamation of Point Grey and South Vancouver into the City of Vancouver. By and large, most members of these municipal forces were taken into the Vancouver force at reasonably adjusted ranks.

Technically, the Force has always been a leader: a 'Rogue's Gallery' of criminal's photographs was begun in 1902; police call boxes were installed on utility poles in 1906, allowing the beat patrolmen more flexibility in covering their areas; the Mounted Squad began in 1907 with three horses, but the first motor vehicle was added in the same year; the first set of fingerprints was taken in September, 1908 (Scotland Yard had made the first successful use of fingerprints in a 1902 case); the first policewomen in North America to be granted the powers of Constable and to conduct street patrols appeared in 1912; the chain gang, which left the jail daily to perform public works hard labour, was abolished as inhumane in 1917 (it lasted much longer in America); 1920 saw the birth of the Identification Squad, whose duties eventually fell to the Crime Lab; mobile radios, after a free trial period, were installed on all five police cars in 1932; after much additional progress, on-board computers appeared in all cars in 1975, for the first time in Canada.

As of December 31, 1993, the Vancouver Police Force consisted of 1131 sworn officers, 107 of whom were female, and 267.5 civilian staff, including part-timers, all but 20 to 25 of whom were female. 55 visible minority members have been drawn mainly from the Native Indian, Japanese, Chinese, Black and Indo-Canadian sectors of the community. The Force operates 225 cars of all types, 34 motorcycles, 28 paddy wagons, vans and trailers (for the Mounted Squad), one police boat and two vintage vehicles. Its active animal complement stood at 17 dogs and seven horses. Its consolidated budget was nearly $92.8 million.

Prisons in British Columbia

The number of jails in B.C. had grown significantly since 1858 but while some of these were dignified by the title 'provincial,' they were mostly small, local and unsuitable for more than overnight drunks and short-term prisoners – 'Thirty dollars or thirty days!' By the mid-1880s, it was apparent that larger permanent facilities were needed.

The B.C. Penitentiary

The Pen, as it was most commonly known, opened in September of 1887. Situated on 65.5 acres rising above the north shore of the Fraser River, approximately one kilometre east of the Patullo Bridge in New Westminster, it was, especially in its final form, an imposing structure. Many a local child, seeing it for the first time from the Fraser Highway near Whalley, has surely mistaken it for a castle. But its crenellated gate block and 30-foot high wall stretching nearly 700 feet on each side have never had anything of glamour about them.

From an inmate population of 23, it rose, in occasional bursts of criminal activity, to an all-time high of 800 in 1961.

The first and last hanging conducted in a federal prison occurred here in 1913, as the result of the murder of a guard during an attempted escape. All other executions have taken place in the provincial jail at Oakalla.

Information on the Pen is generally sketchy, but it had its share of suicides, escapes and riots.

The most notable Pen escapee was Bill Miner, who escaped with three other inmates in 1907 by digging under the brickyard fence. Canada's only train robber, Miner was portrayed in the 1982 film, *The Grey Fox.* His gang had robbed a Canadian Pacific train near Kamloops in 1906, but were soon caught. Miner had been sentenced to life for earlier crimes, and he finally died in a Georgia prison in 1931, but not before he had escaped from five prisons.

As the Pen aged, it became more and more out of step with modern trends in penology, and mere changes in routine could start trouble. Over-crowding has always been the major internal problem of most prisons. After nearly twenty years of relative peace, the truce was broken with a riot and hostage-taking in 1963, hostage incidents again in 1972 and 1975, when one of sixteen hostages died. In terms of physical damage, the riot of 1975 destroyed over 200 cells in the East Wing, most of which were never re-opened.

But with the opening of Kent in 1979, pressures were reduced and the last remaining inmates were quietly transferred to other institutions by February 15, 1980.

The Pen closed it doors on May 10, 1980; only the Main Gate block remains to remind us of its sombre past.

The Oakalla Prison Farm

On May 23, 1911, prompted by the over-crowding of the Pen, the provincial government called for tenders for the construction of a prison farm on 185 acres situated to the northeast of the intersection of Royal Oak Avenue and Oakland Street in Burnaby. The prison was to house those men and women sentenced to less than two years, to hold those persons awaiting trial for serious crimes or appealing federal sentences, and to provide a place of execution for all those condemned to death within the province.

The original main jail was completed in 1914 and contained 160 regular cells and six punishment cells. Employing the Auburn system from America, it was considered to be a model of modern penal practice. In reality, this system, which imposed harsh daytime discipline on prisoners at 'hard labour,' (that term stuck for years in the courts and newspapers, even after both the 'hard' and the 'labour' had disappeared) was unable to reform many of those who did time in Oakalla; it was far better at breeding dissent amongst its inmates and training them for futures in crime. It was typical of many of the prisons of its day – and in these ways, not unlike its shiny modern counterparts.

Over the decades, its population became overcrowded; at its peak, the daily count reached more than 1200 prisoners. Nearly 400 suicides were attempted; less than twenty succeeded. Riots, fired by complaints about the food, living conditions and treatment broke out on several occasions. The most serious riot was that of November 22, 1983, when order was only restored by the appearance of a fully-armed, thirty-two man RCMP Emergency Response Team. The cost from vandalism and minor fires exceeded $150,000, making it twice as expensive as any previous riot.

The grimmest of Oakalla's statistics are the forty-four executions which took place inside its walls between 1919 and 1959. The last execution in Canada took place in 1962.

Escape is foremost in the minds of all prisoners, and Oakalla lost, for various periods of time, at least 890 inmates. The 1988 New Year's Eve escape saw thirteen dangerous prisoners escape from a segregation unit, the infamous 'Hole,' beneath the old cow barn.

In the North American prison subculture, each inmate has the right to wear a tattoo near the web of his thumb. Some are unique to one institution, whereas others are just a general indicator that someone has done time. The tattoo, which isn't compulsory, provides an easy recognition sign between former inmates; woe betide any parolee who has his removed – or any pretender who wears one he is not entitled to. The basic shape in B.C. is an upright cross, called the 'Juvie cross,' which may be acquired when a juvenile first runs afoul of the law. Additional dots around the cross proclaim an inmate's seniority. A tear-drop beside the eye indicates that the wearer has killed someone. These practises continue today in the newer institutions.

By the 1970s, it was obvious that renovations were of no help, so plans were made to construct new facilities elsewhere and to close Oakalla. The closure was completed on June 30, 1991. It is ironic that Oakalla and the Pen, once the least desirable of residences, have now become the sites for hundreds of prestigious townhouses and apartments. Perhaps the new residents will have the time to enjoy the spectacular views that the former residents could not.

Replacement Facilities

In 1991 - 92, the Correctional Service of Canada employed 1647 people in managing 1173 male and 24 female inmates at 9 B.C. locations. Most federal institutions are located in the eastern Fraser Valley. The principal facilities are Mountain and Kent near Agassiz and Ferndale near Mission; they are maximum-, medium- and minimum-security institutions, respectively. Mission, Matsqui and William Head near Victoria are medium security institutions, while Sumas is a community corrections centre. The maximum security Regional Psychiatric Centre in Chilliwack conducts the assessments which were once done in the Forensic Psychiatric Unit at Riverview, as part of the old provincial mental hospital, Essondale, was later known.

During the 1980s, Oakalla was replaced by the Fraser Regional Correctional Centre in Maple Ridge, the Burnaby Correctional Centre for Women and the Surrey and Vancouver Pretrial Services Centres. These, along with other older provincial facilities, such as the Pine Ridge Camp in Maple Ridge, complete the general picture.

We will now turn our attention to the criminals and the crimes which brought them to these and similar places.

The Happy Lion and The Bear

Soldiering is said to consist of long stretches of boredom interrupted by brief moments of sheer terror. Police work is much the same. Thankfully, there aren't really that many frightening episodes in it, but they are made up for by periods of intense activity, and there is no escape from the often grim nature of the work. I joined the Vancouver Police Department on May 1, 1950. I spent three years walking the beat, mainly on Skid Road, followed by five years in the jail and as a Court officer. Outside again, I served in patrol cars for two years before going back inside to the Communications Section, where I was promoted to Corporal. In 1964, I was promoted to Detective, with the equal rank of Sergeant, and joined the Morality Squad. Nick Lohin, my partnersince 1969, had followed a somewhat similar path over 17 years.

Within Morality, we were the General Investigation squad and were assigned to follow up on those cases that could not be completed by uniformed officers. As such, we always had assignments, but emergencies took precedence over everything else. We were mainly concerned with murders, rapes, indecent assaults, robbery and general assaults. Murders, of course, drew out the Homicide squad, but we might also respond to these calls.

Most days begin routinely. We had begun in the usual manner, by logging in at Headquarters at 312 Main Street, just north of Hastings Street, and checking to see whether anyone in the previous shifts had sent anything our way for follow-up. On Friday, June 2, 1972, there was nothing new for us at our 6:00 pm check-in, so we got on the road. It was a nice early summer evening, warm and dry, and the rush-hour traffic had given way to the theatre and party crowd but everything was still moving smoothly.

The police radio is always busy, with cars being assigned to fresh incidents ranging from family disputes, which can quickly become as violent as any other kind of crime, to rapes and murders. The radio system consisted of two channels, one reserved for the downtown core, where most of the activity was concentrated, and another for what is called 'the district,' which is the mostly residential remainder of the city. Friday nights generate a lot of radio traffic from all areas.

At about 8:00, our radio crackled with an odd message: 'Car 20, Car 20, Call the Duty Inspector's office right away.' The dispatcher put me through promptly to the Duty Inspector, who ordered us to join the search for a seven-year old girl who had been missing all day.

The search was being run temporarily from Charles Dickens School at Fifteenth Avenue and Glen Drive, the girl's destination that morning. When we arrived at the school, it was bedlam; there were cars everywhere. Numerous search parties had been organized amongst Cub, Scout and Venturer packs, CB radio clubs and both on- and off-duty policemen. We spoke to the Principal, who was the civilian search co-ordinator, and to the ranking police officer present. We visited the parents, Mr. and Mrs. Klaus Busch, at their home in the 3000-block of Clark Drive. Busch was a guard at the B.C. Penitentiary. He said that they had prepared Tanya for school and that she had left at approximately 8:30 am, carrying her red plastic lunch kit and a library book titled *The Happy Lion and The Bear.* Tanya was dressed in a white sweater with a Munich Olympics medallion attached to the zipper pull. She had on a white blouse, a red plaid skirt, bobby socks and black shoes. A full missing person report had already been phoned in to headquarters. Neither parent was able to offer an explanation for her disappearance. They could not believe that she had stopped anywhere on the way or had gone with any friend as children sometimes do. We continued the investigation ourselves with very little results. We could not find anybody who had seen Tanya reach the school. We worked well into the morning hours with no results.

At 8:00 Saturday morning, we reported to Headquarters, where we were officially assigned to the case. Bill Snowden, the Sergeant in charge, had just transferred out of the Intelligence Unit and quickly arranged to put a tap on the Busch's phone. As all things pointed to it being a kidnapping, we felt we might yet receive a phone call. He organized the tedious details of a house-to-house search, centred on the 3000 block Clark Drive and extending for several miles in all directions. We were prepared to search all the houses and apartments in Vancouver if we had to, but of course, such a vast search would have taken many days. The searchers asked each householder for permission to quickly search their house and garage for the missing child. When permission was granted, the searcher would do a quick walk-through search, including a look in all closets and storage spaces. There were no outright refusals but many houses had to be visited twice or more in order to find someone at home. A warrant was never needed; people were more than co-operative. It takes a great deal of evidence to obtain a search warrant but a bit of talking goes a long way. This search netted us a lady who lived opposite the school who recalled a similarly described girl coming out of the school yard at approximately 8:45 am. There could have been a man with her, but she could not be certain as her view was partially blocked, but she did recall the girl leaving. Meanwhile, all the searchers' reports of found articles were checked out. There were hundreds of people involved in the search. We asked for and got a list of all known sex offenders in the Lower Mainland; several of these were still in custody, but the remainder were systematically checked out with the assistance of Detectives Joe Stanton and George Johnson of the Morality Squad.

Monday morning brought us the first really useful information, when one of Tanya's classmates, who had been away for the weekend, returned to school. She knew nothing of Tanya's disappearance until she reached school that morning. She said she had seen Tanya leave the far end of school yard with her lunch bucket and library book. She was with a man, whom she described as best she could remember, as a white male with bushy hair, approximately 25 years of age. They both got into a car parked at the corner of Inverness and Fifteenth and drove away.

The days went by, and although many suspects were checked out, and the searchers had increased to the thousands and the search area had spread ever-wider, it was all to no avail. By this time, various organizations and individuals had offered rewards totalling $4500 for information leading to Tanya Busch's whereabouts.

Lohin and I met frequently with the search supervisors, discussing our progress with them, and we kept them posted on what we believe happened and what we were looking for. The unsolved murder of seven-year old Evangeline Azarcon came to everyone's mind. She had disappeared while on her way home from Edith Cavell School at 19th and Heather on November 20, 1969. In January of 1970, her body was found in a shallow pond near 192nd Street and 98th Avenue, near the east end of Barnston Island, in the Port Kells area. She had been sexually molested. No useable clues were found and the case was still unsolved.

We received many calls from concerned citizens and all were investigated. Late in the day, a member of the Pen staff called to report that an inmate, Charles David Garry Head, who was out on a weekend pass, had called at the main gate about noon on Friday, asking to see a psychiatrist. Head was serving a 15-year sentence for the rape of a seven-year old child.

Charlie Head had a rather short record but it was brutal. He first came to RCMP attention in Surrey in February of 1965, for causing a disturbance and wilful damage; as a first offender, he received a light fine and a six month suspended sentence on a $200.00 bond and was required to make restitution. In April of 1967, he was charged with buggery and gross indecency but a stay of proceedings was entered; one month later he was convicted and sentenced on one count each of rape (life), attempted rape (ten years concurrent), and indecent assault on a seven-year old female (five years concurrent). His lawyer launched a successful appeal in June of 1967 on the rape charge and the sentence was reduced to 15 years but the other convictions were upheld. By the end of October, 1967, the Crown's application for a preventive detention order as a dangerous sexual offender had been granted, to replace the five year sentence for indecent assault imposed in May. Head was now thoroughly enmeshed in the penal system, and would leave a considerable paper trail behind him.

On June 8, detectives Stanton and Johnson interviewed Head in the Pen, questioning him about his movements on June 2. He had been serving time in the Agassiz Mountain Prison, approximately 80 miles from Vancouver, and had been released on a four-day 'rehabilitation' pass on Thursday June 1. His story was that he had been with friends in Surrey between 8:00 and 9:00 on the morning of Friday June 2. Helen and James Groves, whom Head claimed he'd been with on that morning, immediately told the investigators that he had come to see them three times on June 2, but all much later in the day than he claimed. On June 9, Lohin and I re-interviewed Head in the Pen. He gave us a written statement, in which he used the same alibi, unaware that it had already been broken. He also claimed to have met aand made a deal with a well-known drug trafficker. We had never seen Head before, so we looked him over pretty thoroughly, and we noticed that the hair on his head had been cut very recently. He had lost his right eye somewhere along the way and the false eye allowed him to appear to be looking at you when he really wasn't. There was noticeable unrest in the Pen once the inmates and the guards learned from the grapevine that we were there to interview Head about the abduction of Tanya Busch. Crime is crime, and perhaps the only vestige of 'honour among thieves' is their nearly universal hatred of child molesters, known as skinners, and child murderers.

With the warden's permission, we transferred Head to our cells in Vancouver. During the drive in, I rather casually asked Head if he'd take us to where he'd left Tanya Busch. Head refused. We promptly held a line-up but Tanya's young classmate was unable to identify anyone in it. The Vancouver City Police polygraph expert was away, so we arranged for Corporal Les Holmes of the RCMP to perform the polygraph tests at their Heather Street barracks, on 33rd Avenue west of Cambie Street. When we got to the polygraph room, Head said, "I'm not taking any polygraph test." I said to him, "You are an inmate of the B.C. Pen. You have the chance here to clear yourself of any knowledge in the disappearance of Tanya Busch. You are refusing to do so. You realize that you are going to be returned to the Pen and that you are the main suspect in this case." "Yeah," he replied, " But I'm not taking the test." It is often difficult to remain calm; I snapped at Head, "You son of a bitch; you killed her and we'll prove it!" I didn't realize I'd said this until the tape, which had been running from the time we had entered the polygraph room, was played back to me later. All such tests were taped; currently, many police departments are starting to video tape all suspect interviews. A Vancouver City Police supervisor, who will remain nameless, offered to take Head into a room and get a confession for us. That made me angry again! "If you so much as touch him, I'll have you locked up! You lay a hand on him and we'll all end up in the Pen trading him places." I am amazed that people who know better fall into that stupid trap. One of the prerequisites for the job is the ability to remain calm, rational and methodical in distressful situations. Emotion doesn't solve crimes. The return trip to the Pen was made in a quiet but unfriendly atmosphere.

Nonetheless, we felt that we had a very likely suspect and our task was now to determine if he could have done it, and ultimately, whether he had actually done it.

Mrs. Head told us that Garry had driven her to work in New Westminster in her car prior to 8:00 am and that he had then driven away in it. We asked the Surrey RCMP to seize it and we began a thorough examination of it and its contents for evidence. RCMP Constable Seefried and Corporals Anderson and Erickson were assigned to assist us. We sought and obtained a search warrant for Mrs. Head's house in Surrey. Mrs. Head told us, "If my son killed that little girl, they should hang him. If it will help, I'll stay away and you can search the house to your heart's content." It would seem that he had caused his mother a great deal of unhappiness that did not show up in police records.

We searched the house in a particularly painstaking manner. Corporal Joe Mikita of the Vancouver Identification Squad arrived and took samples of human hair from the house, as well as fur from the tortoise shell cat, which was black, white and orange in colour. On Head's bedsheet, we observed what appeared to be blood. The bed also yielded an 8-inch long blonde hair. In the yard, a septic tank buckled as someone drove over it; the RCMP got the unpleasant job of draining and filtering the sludge in the tank searching for a body. The property consisted of five acres and every square foot had to be carefully logged off as having been inspected and found empty of items of possible interest or, failing that, the description and position of any interesting materials noted. Our police dog searched it thoroughly and all the adjoining properties as well, while the RCMP dog searched further afield, all without results. The neighbours were questioned but very little was gained this way. The Pen staff confirmed that Head had appeared at the Pen gate at about noon on June 2, asking to see a psychiatrist, or at least, trying to make an a appointment to see one. He realized that if he was going to establish an alibi, very few people would know him, as he had spent the past five years in prison, but the Pen staff were familiar with him.

As the days passed, Lohin and I decide to search the area around the Head place again, although Detectives Stanton and Johnson had also searched the area earlier, as had other officers. The area was generally heavily wooded, and extensive blackberry thickets grew in the more open spaces between the trees, making it very difficult to enter and conduct an effective search. On several occasions, we ran into a middle-aged woman with several dogs; she asked us to look for the body of one of her dogs, which she felt had died somewhere in this area.

On June 14, we set out to trace the probable route that Head could have taken from Dickens School to his mother's house. The intervening twelve days since the abduction had been warm and dry. All we knew for certain was that Tanya had been abducted at approximately 8:45. Head was back at the Pen gate by noon. At 8:45, Lohin and I left the schoolyard at 15th and Inverness, drove north on Glen Drive to 12th Avenue and turned east, travelling over the Grandview Highway and onto Highway 401. We drove at or below the posted speed limit at all times, and respected yellow traffic lights by stopping, rather than hurrying through the intersections. We turned off 401 at the 160th Street off-ramp, proceeded north to 108th Avenue and stopped in front of the Head house. It had taken us approximately twenty minutes to travel eighteen miles; this left almost three hours to be accounted for. Too much time to rule out foul play. After considering these things for some time, we left the house and drove east on 108th Avenue to 168th Street, where I told Nick to turn left towards the Fraser

River. The road was very rough and there were no houses to break up the stretches of dense bush. We drove deeper down the road, although this area had been searched earlier by Stanton, Johnson, the Surrey police dog and his handler. The bush crowded closer to the rotten road, leaning over the ditches to almost touch the car. We stopped and got out. The weather had changed, and the air was very still. As we walked slowly down this road, looking carefully into the bush on either side, I felt that I had been here before, almost as if I had seen this road in a dream. We had walked some way closer to the river when I said, "Nick, can you smell that?" The most unpleasant memory of police life is that sickly sweet smell of death, we could both smell it; as we'd smelled it many times before. Nick looked at me and said, "Yes, I don't think it's the lady's dead dog we're smelling." I took out a Kleenex and tore it into strips; the air, so calm before, had begun to stir with the first signs of impending rain. The odour stung at us and the Kleenex turned in towards the bush, just the slightest bit to one side. I stood there pointing into the bush, while Nick jumped the ditch and fought through the blackberry thorns. At about fifty feet, he said, "I've found her body!" It was barely ten o'clock. God, we'd rather have found that it was the dog.

I left him there, with instructions to keep everybody out except myself, and I walked hurriedly back down the road past the car. For secrecy, I decided to use a phone rather than the radio; we didn't want reporters and other CB-scanning curiosity-seekers arriving before the forensic team. I immediately wondered whether I'd made the right choice, as our civilian employees were then on strike and I had a lot of difficulty getting through and being put on hold, but I finally reached Sergeant Snowden, who sensed the unusual, and began asking me direct questions:

"Did you find her?"

"Yes," I said.

"Where are you?"

"108th Avenue and 168th Street in Surrey. Send Mikita and the van."

I then phoned Staff Sergeant Wally Gorgopa of the Surrey RCMP, who went through the same routine, questioning me so that I could repeat the same short answers again. The lady of the house knew from my expression that something was very wrong, but politely or fearfully, she didn't ask any questions.

I went back outside to wait. A young Surrey RCMP Constable was the first to arrive. I introduced myself, asked his name, wrote it down and turned to face him squarely.

"We've found the body of a young girl who has been murdered down the road. You see that big blonde fellow there; that's Nick Lohin, Detective Nick Lohin, Vancouver Police: he's my partner. Now, you; you are not to let anybody down that road. I don't care if it's your superintendent or mine – nobody. I'm holding you responsible for not letting anyone down that road until I say so." He was good; he obeyed me explicitly.

We waited while police car after police car arrived. Staff Sergeant Gorgopa came to ask what I needed; 'Just to keep everybody out of there, that's all." He repeated my instructions to his young Constable, adding his own emphasis. Gorgopa said his own science squad would arrive shortly. Snowden and Mikita arrived in our Identification van. After what seemed like a very long wait, the New Westminster Coroner and a doctor arrived. The Constable referred them promptly to me and I let them pass through. Everyone else, the press and what-have-you, were kept well back. At 11:15, the doctor confirmed that she was dead. After an annoying two-hour wait, the RCMP Identification van arrived, after a fashion; just two officers, two cameras and a shoe box for collecting evidence! Technically, we had to ask permission to set up our own equipment because we were in RCMP territory.

By now, there were approximately fifty RCMP officers on hand, all young and eager, wearing coveralls. Inspector Riddle formed them into a skirmish line and they went into the brush, practically on their hands and knees. The brush was so thick that when a man tripped and fell, he never reached the ground but was held up by the sharp blackberry brambles. I told Inspector Riddle that I was looking for Tanya's lunch kit and the library book. Riddle's crew searched the bush repeatedly, working their way in and out to the road again, until they were exhausted but found nothing unusual or useful.

I approached the body again. I was uncomfortable, both angry and sad. A quick glance was enough to see that it must be Tanya, as the girl was neatly dressed according to the description, right down to the Olympic medallion on her sweater.

The ambulance attendants came in with a sterile body tube to remove the remains. This is standard procedure for all murders and cases of suspicious deaths; it ensures that the contents of the tube pertain solely to the investigation in hand, and that anything later found in the tube was placed there during body removal; such evidence may be crucial.

With the body was removed, Nick and I helped in the search. When the general search ended, Riddle walked slowly in towards the body site, which had not yet been thoroughly scanned and found a piece of silk stocking, which he gave to Constable Seefried, the Evidence Officer. On all major investigations, an Evidence Officer is designated; he records in his notebook all the evidence found for later presentation in court. This material was similar to that in stockings we had seen in the Head house, and another found closer to the body site. Riddle then ordered the area searched again, and this took several more hours.

Johnson, Stanton, Corporal Erickson and I drove to the Pen. Johnson and Stanton found Klaus Busch , who had just started back to work again, and told him of his daughter's fate. Meanwhile, Erickson and I questioned Head once again. He was expecting us, as he'd heard on the radio that the body had been found and he would not say anything.

We now turned the case over to the RCMP. We gave them copies of everything, from the initial missing child report, every suspect interview and the final report on how we'd found the body.

By now, the case had reached the House of Commons, where MPs were angry at the thought of an offender on a weekend pass murdering a little girl.

No Comment (from *The Sun*, June 14/72)

In response to a series of pointed questions by Eldon Woolliams, (Conservative, Calgary North) Solicitor-General Jean-Pierre Goyer rose in the Commons Thursday and expressed his deepest sympathy to Tanya's parents and said he is investigating the matter. Woolliams, the justice critic in the Conservative opposition, asked the Minister in the House of Commons about the report in Wednesday's *Province* that a prisoner who had been on temporary leave from Agassiz Mountain Prison was being questioned in connection with the death. Goyer, who has been something of a crusader for penal reform and recently unveiled a plan that would allow inmates to be boarded out with old-age pensioners, said he would not comment on the reports surrounding the girl's death until the RCMP inquiry is complete. He told Woolliams, who is one of Alberta's top criminal lawyers, that he has asked the Commissioner of Penitentiaries and the National Parole Board for a report on a convict who may be implicated in her death.

Woolliams continued to tackle the Minister on the entire system of temporary leaves. He said several reports from across the country indicated that a number of prisoners given temporary leave disappear.

"I think we are entitled to know how this system is working, particularly as there seems to be some suggestion of foul play in reference to Tanya Busch." he said. Goyer replied that he had commented on the leave program several times. "In almost 100 percent of the releases, there were no problems. Only a very small percentage of inmates released caused trouble." he said.

Woolliams, however, said it was all very well for the Minister to talk about the success rate, but what about the unsuccessful cases?

"Particularly when a man has been convicted of a sexual offence, we must be very careful in granting him temporary leave. Surely, this latest incident brings into question the whole method of the screening system. We know that psychiatrists are involved in these cases, but psychiatry isn't an exact science. Obviously, increased screening is called for."

In addition to Woolliams' partisan questions, four B.C. Liberal MPs have recommended to the Solicitor-General that weekend passes for sex criminals be cancelled. Jerry Pringle (Fraser Valley East) said the recommendation was meant to stand only if an inmate was charged in the slaying of seven-year old Tanya Busch. Pringle said the recommendation was made when he and three other Liberal MPs, Tom Goode, Veterans' Affairs Minister Art Laing and Grant Deachman, asked for a meeting with Goyer following the discovery Wednesday of the little girl's body in Surrey bushland.

"We don't want to be judge and jury in this case, but we are concerned." said Pringle. He said the group recommended that if the man is charged, there be an immediate suspension of the passes, and the whole question of the weekend passes be studied.

Outside the House, Woolliams said that if it should come to light that a convict was involved, the whole system of granting temporary leave should be reviewed. Meanwhile, RCMP continued to question a young sex offender who was reported to have been out on a four-day pass from Agassiz Mountain Prison when Tanya was abducted. He said that it had also been suggested that the inmate now under suspicion was actually in jail for a sexual offence and perhaps even a previous sex-slaying.

Sadly, crimes of this sort can and do still occur; on October 24, 1992, 16-year old Jason Gamache, a parolee who had been previously been convicted of child molesting, raped and brutally murdered six-year old Dawn Shaw in Courtenay.

Such a repetition raise several important questions. Firstly, while admitting that psychiatry is an inexact science, it seems that no progress has been made in the intervening twenty years towards either 'curing' such offenders or in determining whether they are 'safe' enough to be given some freedom. 'Cured' and 'safe' are dangerously vague terms at best. Secondly, in the age of instantaneous communications, how is it possible that a parolee, whose parole had very definite and stringent conditions attached to it, can simply move from town to town without any notice being given to the new police force that he was now in their territory? Gamache was barred from having unsupervised contact with children, but he frequently baby-sat and played with children in his new neighbourhood; he even baby-sat the siblings of his victim while the distraught parents visited the police station! He had previously admitted similar breaches of parole to his parole officer, who had "...learned to trust the polite high-school athlete." Crap! Who will stand up and defend the practices which cost this child her life? Everyone, whether parolee or honest citizen, has to earn their privileges by progressively demonstrating that they are, in fact, ready for them. Neither Charlie Head nor Jason Gamache were ready...they never will be and society needs to be protected from them.

On June 15, we met with Inspector Thompson at the Surrey RCMP Headquarters. Thompson had just been assigned to the case. We met again a few days later and found to our dismay that Thompson was still sending his men out over trails that we had proven to be dead ends. He didn't seem to believe that we had the right man. What a strange turn of events. A couple of RCMP Constables told us that they'd been searching for Head's clothing and personal effects for a week at Agassiz Mountain without success. Erickson and I looked at each other in disgust. Our report on Head began by stating that his personal effects were in the Warden's office at the Pen! Other officers complained of repeatedly crawling on their hands and knees through the Head yard, searching for the Olympic medallion. My mind filled with the image Tanya's body in the brambles, with the medallion, still prominently displayed on her sweater! At this point, Inspector Thompson was ordering his men to check new suspects who just might be responsible, and I interrupted to ask, "Don't you think that finding the body so close to the Head house makes him a prime suspect?"

Thompson ignored me; he was going to conduct his own investigation, regardless of our efforts.

So we decided to continue with *our* investigation. Lohin and I went to the Royal Columbian Hospital and Nick went to the morgue in the basement and obtained several strands of hair from Tanya's head, which we gave to Ted Fennell and Alec Beatton. They were our police analysts in those days and were amongst the best in their field. Although matching hair characteristics was not considered as positive an identification as a fingerprint, the strong similarities of the two samples would have to be argued against by the defence counsel. For this reason, I refused an order from a supervisor, who shall remain nameless, to take the samples to the Bellingham office of the FBI so that they could do a more thorough comparison. This way, the element of doubt would have to be removed by the defence, whereas the FBI just might weaken our case with an unfavourable comparison. Our Superintendent was present at the time and did not overrule my refusal.

The RCMP investigators did add important facets to the case. They found one of the Head's neighbours who, on the morning of June 2, saw someone drive up about 9:30 and enter the Head house. A neighbour lady who kept dogs (not the one we met near the body) remembered that her dogs began to howl just prior to 11 o'clock that morning. She felt it was very weird because she had never heard dogs howl that loudly before. We now guessed that was the time of Tanya's death.

An adult witness and a child had seen the Head car pass by with a female in the passenger's seat. Three inmates of the Pen came forward to present evidence in the case. There may be little honour among thieves but all criminals unite in their hatred of child murderers, and when opportunities have presented themselves, they have acted upon their own to deal out rough justice. Speaking out in such a case is not considered 'squealing.'

On June 25, 1972, the RCMP charged 26-year old Charles David Garry Head with non-capital murder. Raymond Paris appeared in Head's defence, while Allan

Cliffe, a Vancouver City Assistant Prosecutor, presented the Crown's case in the preliminary hearing before Mr. Justice Thomas Keenleyside of the B.C. Supreme Court on November 1. The evidence, while circumstantial, was overwhelming. The strand of hair from the bed was a close match to Tanya's and the fibrous material in the trunk of Head's car matched that of the stockings found in the house and at the body site.

The three inmates gave evidence. It was discovered that Head bore a grudge against Busch over a minor detail, so minor that when Busch was questioned about it, he could not even remember anything other than the two of them having words over something. It should have been nothing serious, but it seemed to grow and fester in Head's mind. One prisoner stated that Head said he could never confess to the murder because his mother and grandmother would lose faith in him and the Parole Board would never trust him again; recall his mother's earlier comment. The next inmate said that during June of 1972, while he was in the Protective Custody Unit at the Pen, he'd had a discussion with Charlie Head, who had just been brought back from Agassiz Mountain Prison:

> "Head was locked in his cell at the Protective Custody Unit. I went over and asked him why they had brought him back from camp. Head replied, 'Over that Busch deal.' Later on, Head invited me to his cell because he wanted to talk. I asked him if they had anything on him for the Busch murder; 'They've got fuck all,' Head said. I told him that a guy should kill a snake like Busch (in reality, few prison guards are liked by the prisoners, even if they are fair) instead of an innocent kid. Head said, 'People who enjoy making others suffer should be made to suffer themselves; you don't kill them.' I looked at Head and asked, 'Charlie, did you kill that kid?' Head replied in a low voice, 'Yeah, I killed her.' He showed no regrets but looked like he enjoyed remembering it. We talked for another five minutes about the Agassiz camp and then I left."

At the conclusion of the hearing, Judge Keenleyside committed Head for trial on a charge of non-capital murder in the death of Tanya Busch.

Capital murder was defined as the murder of a police officer or prison guard who was acting in the normal course of his duties; non-capital murder covered the murder of all other persons. Death sentences continued to be pronounced until 1969, even though the last execution had taken place in 1962. Head knew that he was risking only his freedom, not his life, by murdering Tanya.

Defence Counsel Paris argued successfully for a change of venue and the trial was thus scheduled to be held in Quesnel, before Mr. Justice Thomas Berger of the B.C. Supreme Court. Mr. H. Lee Skipp of Williams Lake now became the chief prosecutor, assisted by Allan Cliffe. During the preliminary hearing, twenty-eight Crown witnesses had appeared, and another seven were named but not called. The sheer volume of testimony clearly demonstrates why court cases of any kind cost so much; we as taxpayers must pay for this somehow.

In the trial itself, which began on January 22, 1973, a total of twenty-six prosecution witnesses were called:

4 Vancouver Police Officers,
4 RCMP members,
2 Minors (unsworn), Tanya Busch's classmates,
7 Neighbours and acquaintances of the accused,
5 Technical experts, including the Coroner, two doctors, and a psychiatrist,
3 Inmates, 1 each from the Pen, Agassiz Mountain and Matsqui Prison, and
1 Drug dealer.

The defence called only three witnesses; a psychiatrist, the Pen Records Officer and Surrey RCMP Corporal Anderson.

The well-known drug dealer appeared and swore that he did not know any person by the name of Garry Head (or various aliases thereof; Head's prison friends called him Charlie but most of his outside contacts called him Garry), did not make arrangements to meet any person in Burnaby on June 2 nor had he ever seen the accused before appearing in court. When cross-examined, he admitted that he had a long police record, mainly for drug-related offences.

One of the inmates testified that, approximately a year before the murder, Head had said that he knew how to murder a person so that the cause of death could not be determined. Head had claimed, he said, that holding his hand tightly over the victim's mouth and nose would cause them to lapse into unconsciousness and they would then die within a few minutes. Furthermore, Head had added that he would kill his next victim so that she could not testify against him.

Oddly, the testimony of two of the defence witnesses, Mr. Farrance, the Pen Records Officer, and RCMP Cpl. Anderson, pertained to the disappearance of Evangeline Azarcon, not that of Tanya Busch; the Crown never raised the Azarcon case, as it had yielded even fewer clues than this one and nothing but 'hearsay' had ever linked Head to it. There was no obvious connection between the crimes other than the similarity of victims and the short distance separating the sites where the bodies were found. Dr. McDonald, the psychiatrist, who had examined Head at intervals between August 1967 and July 1971, said that Head phoned during the morning of June 2 and later visited his West Broadway office at about 2:15pm. While of the opinion that Head had exhibited some forms of compulsive sexual behaviour in the past, he recalled that Head was quite calm and undisturbed during this visit and that he had given no indication of any substantial problems at the time.

During his cross-examination, Defence Counsel Paris confronted one of the inmates: "You've been convicted of robbery, drug offences, breaking and entering...but the inmate, catching the drift of this attack, interrupted him, saying, "Yes, I have; but I don't murder seven-year old girls." Paris changed his line of questioning; the jury couldn't miss the inmate's message.

The three inmate witnesses were always troublesome. Just picking them up and transporting them to and from court appearances turned a couple of officers into chauffeurs for the day. While they were credible witnesses, they were often too 'street-smart' for our purposes; on the journey back from the preliminary hearing, two of them told their chauffeurs that they hadn't told all they knew about the murder. Why the hell not? A day in court, when it doesn't add to your own sentence, is a holiday from prison boredom and sometimes you just might see someone you don't like get his come-uppance. Because they could be vindictive, their evidence had to reviewed very carefully.

And they like to escape. Between the preliminary hearing and the trial, one of them escaped from Agassiz Mountain. Before his capture at dawn the next day, he had committed seven major offences, including abduction, indecent assault and rape. These earned him some 34 additional years in confinement and a life sentence that is not 'easy time.' What strange people; when interviewed after his arrest, he seemed to bear no ill feelings towards us and assured us that he'd be glad to testify against Head at the Spring assizes. And he did.

One of the inmates, who had actually finished serving his time a week before the trial began, was kept in protective custody under a Material Witness Warrant. After cross-examination, he was released on parole in Quesnel. Of course, the only people he knew in chilly Quesnel, so unlike balmy Vancouver, were police officers connected with the case and he ended up drinking with detectives Johnson and Stanton until 11:30 pm, when he wandered over to the bus station to consider the long ride home. In the station, he was recognized by Jon Wilson, editor of *The Cariboo Observer*. Wilson, hoping to capitalize on the most important trial of the year, invited him back to the newspaper office where they drank, discussed the murder case and traded yarns until about 5:30 am. At this point, Wilson left to find the local RCMP, who brought him and the parolee before the Court in due order.

It seems that the parolee had told Wilson that the trio had conspired to manufacture false evidence against Head to ensure his conviction. The parolee, who had been re-arrested on another Material Witness Warrant, maintained that his original evidence was genuine, that he had been drunk when talking to Wilson, that the more interesting his stories were, the more generously Wilson poured and that he couldn't recall much of what he and Wilson had talked about anyway. The other inmates were re-sworn and again maintained that their evidence was genuine and that they had not discussed the case among themselves. Crown Counsel then called Detective Johnson, who testified that when he and Stanton had parted company with the man at 11:30 the night before, that the parolee was in an advanced state of intoxication and that he, Johnson, would not place any credence on the statements he was alleged to have made later in the morning. Defense Counsel immediately seized on Wilson as a new witness, but was unable to make anything useful out of the incident.

One of Head's neighbours had seen Mrs. Head's car pull into the driveway with Head and a female passenger in it, about 9:20 am one day, but had been somewhat uncertain of the date. At the trial, however, she stated that she had now confirmed that this had taken place on June 2. She had heard a child crying, a door slam and then nothing more. She saw Mrs. Head's car leave at about 10:10 am and proceed east on 108th Avenue. Paris, in his cross-examination, asked why she not given this evidence at the Preliminary Hearing. She replied that at that time she had been unsure of the date, but that she had been writing out a cheque that morning, had answered the phone and, in returning to complete the cheque, had looked out the window and had seen the car arrive. She then produced the cancelled cheque, dated June 2, 1972, which entered as an exhibit. "I am now sure of the date." she said. She also identified Head in the courtroom and Mrs. Head's car from photographs.

Crown Counsel Skipp submitted that there were eleven points of circumstantial evidence, in addition to the strong direct evidence of the inmate/escapee and the neighbour, whose cancelled cheque dated the occurrence so exactly; evidence which proved Head was guilty of the murder. The evidence had shown that Head had prior intent, motive and opportunity to kill the daughter of the man he hated so bitterly. Defense Counsel Paris termed the Crown's case 'strictly circumstantial and mere coincidence,' arguing that there had been no positive identification of Head as the person seen with Tanya, and therefore, that he should be given the benefit of the doubt and be acquitted. We had sought so long in vain for Tanya's lunch kit and library book in the hope that Head had left some fingerprints on them; this would have materially strengthened our case.

Mr. Justice Berger charged the jury during the morning of January 26, 1973, summarizing all the evidence produced in the trial, explaining points of law, especially that of circumstantial evidence, and closed by saying that it was not necessary for the Crown to prove the cause of death in order for them to find the accused guilty. After a deliberation of three hours and ten minutes, the jury brought in a verdict of 'guilty as charged.'

Justice Berger then sentenced Head to life imprisonment. Head had declined to take the stand in his own defense. The expected appeal was heard on February 27, 1973, by Justices Ferris, McLean and Rankin, who unanimously rejected it. To the best of my knowledge, Charlie Head is still, as of April 1994, serving his sentence in the Saskatchewan Penitentiary in Prince Albert.

The case of Evangeline Azarcon, so similar in many ways, is still unsolved. On November 20, 1969, Head was serving time in the Pen; at least, that is what the records say. But it has since been suggested that inmates have access to those records, and it is possible that the records could have been altered. In connection with this inquiry, a different neighbour stated, "I have known Garry Head all my life and on the weekend that Evangeline Azarcon was murdered, I saw him out on a weekend pass. I took my children and pointed him out to them. I told them 'If you ever see that man, if he ever comes near you, you get home and don't go near him!'

As serving officers, Lohin and I would not think of claiming the reward for finding Tanya; it was our job to do it and we did.

The Unfriendly Giant

On October 28, 1968, I reported at headquarters for the day shift at approximately 7:30 am. Staff Sergeant Creech, the duty NCO, handed me one rape and two indecent assault complaints. He said that I probably couldn't do much with the rape as there was no suspect. Nor would the two indecent assaults take too long either. Everything looked slow and unpromising. At this time, I was working alone in the general investigations section of the Morality Squad.

The rape had occurred at Brockton Point in Stanley Park on the previous day, Sunday, at approximately 3 pm. The complainant was a 22-year old woman who had recently moved to Vancouver. The suspect was described as a white male, aged about 35, 180 pounds, medium build, fair complexion, dirty blonde wavy hair, grey eyes, grey bulky knit woollen sweater, perhaps a Cowichan sweater, stretched out of shape and decorated with skiers in red, clean shaven, coarse features, teeth in the top jaw crooked, grey beige sport shirt and wearing dirty running shoes.

I phoned the victim and asked her to come down to headquarters, which she did the next day, Tuesday. She was one of the most beautiful blonde women that I have ever seen. She was six feet tall and beautifully proportioned. She had recently arrived from Germany but spoke very good English. I took out the Morality Mug Book and she started going through it. After only ten pages, she stopped, looking at Douglas Ronald Anderson, who had been released from Oakalla on October 12. "That's him! Without a doubt, that's him!" she said. Anderson's write-up described him as six foot ten and weighing 210 pounds; the original investigating officer had neglected to include the suspect's height, even though the victim insisted that she had mentioned it to him. "How tall was the man who raped you?" I asked. She looked at me and said, "I think you are about 180 centimetres tall. (She was correct; I am five feet eleven) That man was much taller than you," and she reached up as high as she could. "Very tall," she said. I looked at Anderson's mug shot again and said, "Gotcha!" Incredibly, his rap sheet listed him as working just across the street, in a furniture factory at 259 East Cordova. I thanked the young lady, collected PCs Cooper and Raines, and went across the street; it looked like it would be easy. The furniture factory was on the second floor, and as we went up the stairs, we heard a commotion above us. At the head of the stairs, we were met by the owner and the rest of the workmen, who told us that the moment Anderson had seen us approaching the front door, he had run to the back of the shop, jumped some twenty-five feet out a window onto a truck parked in the lane, and escaped northwards on Gore.

We took the names and stories of two witnesses before we left. The owner said that Anderson had tried to borrow money from everyone in the shop that morning, but that no one had given him any, since the previous Friday had been payday. Anderson had phoned that morning and had said he needed some travelling money and wanted his severance cheque mailed to him but, when questioned, he wouldn't say where he wanted it mailed to. The owner refused to go along with this and told Anderson to stop fooling around and come to work. One of the employees told us that on Monday morning, Anderson had told him that he'd met a girl in Stanley Park. As he recalled it, Anderson had said, 'She took me into the bushes, but she had a guy waiting there to roll me. Now I'm broke; can you lend me a few bucks?' The worker refused to help him, saying "It's your own damn fault." At this point, the owner had joined the conversation, and Anderson told him, "It's a long story; best if you don't know about it. Some stupid dame thought she could clip me but she got clipped; I used my hands." So there the matter stood until we appeared on Tuesday morning.

I issued a warrant for Anderson's arrest on a charge of rape. The original investigating Officer's report follows:

'I was summoned to the Chilco bus loop by a radio call. I found R.P. Smith talking to a blonde woman, both seated in the rear of a blue Austin, BC 321-528. As I approached the vehicle, a man stepped forward and introduced himself, his wife and another lady, all from West Vancouver. They had been walking a trail running from the north side of Brockton Point near the MV Beaver memorial cross. This trail runs in an easterly direction and terminates on the Park Drive proper on the south side of the Point. These people saw a young blonde female, naked from the waist down, except for her stockings, who appeared to be in a very agitated mental state. The man's wife approached the woman and asked if she needed help. She described the rest of the victim's clothes as a corduroy jacket, and a blouse with part of a brassiere pulled part of the way through one of the buttonholes in the blouse. The victim told her that a man had been holding her by the throat, had forced her to the ground and had told her not to make any noise or she would be hurt. Accompanied by these people, she returned to the scene of the assault and recovered a pair of shoes, a pair of white lace panties and a pair of corduroy slacks. With some help, the victim re-dressed herself and they led her to their car. They drove through the park, searching for a police officer, eventually finding one at the Chilco bus loop.

'With this background information, I then spoke to the victim, who said that she had entered the Park about noon. She is a new Canadian, recently arrived from Munich, West Germany, and had never been in the Park before. She toured the Zoo area, walked to Beaver Lake and subsequently found herself on the seawall near Siwash Rock.

'By this time, she was completely disoriented, and when the suspect spoke to her, and seemed to be a very friendly sort of person, she told him that she was lost. He said that he would show her the way out of the Park, so they began walking. After some time, she began to grow uneasy about the man but she did not want to cause a scene by telling him to leave. At this time of year, the Park is not well-visited and there were no other people in the vicinity. When she recognized the Totem Poles, she told him that she did not think that this was the way out of the Park, but he said that he was showing her the way back now.

'He led her down the small trail near the stone cross, politely ushering her ahead of himself. They had gone only a short distance when he grabbed from behind with his arm around her throat and forced her to the ground. She tried to persuade him from attacking her on the grounds that someone might find them. He replied, "It's okay; nobody ever uses this path." With his free hand, he tried to undo the buttons of her blouse, reached inside and drew the brassiere over her breasts and pulled it part of the way through one of the buttonholes. He did not rip the brassiere but he had used enough force to tear the metal clasps away from the fabric. She said that he did not otherwise use excessive force and did not bruise or handle her breasts roughly. He turned her on her back, with his hand over her mouth, and said, "Don't scream or something bad will happen..." She was too scared to put up any form of overt resistance but tried unsuccessfully several times to get up from the ground, but the suspect held her down too effectively.

'At this time, he looked very wild and excited. She recalled that he had said to her. "Be nice to me; the girls don't like me." He now removed her slacks and her panties and just opened his pants, so that she saw his penis. He settled her on her back again and had intercourse with her. She said that she was so frightened that she didn't feel anything at all. Just as he began the act, she saw a small dog appear on the trial, followed promptly by two small children, who looked at them and then walked away. She said something, which she now can't remember, to the suspect, who looked up and probably saw the dog and the children. He then jumped up and ran away. She got up and took a few steps, just as the people from West Vancouver appeared. With their help, she re-dressed and they led her to their car and eventually to a police officer.

'When he had first introduced himself, he had said that he was an American; however, due to his shabby appearance and his detailed knowledge of Stanley Park, it would appear that the suspect is a local person and may even be known to the Morality Squad or GIS. The victim is very positive that she can identify him.

'PC Bateman escorted the victim to the stables to await transportation to Saint Paul's Hospital. In the company of Cpl. R.C. West, she arrived at the hospital at 5:10, and departed at 5:50 for her home.'

No trace was found of Anderson at any of his usual Vancouver haunts and his room showed signs of his hurried packing; it seemed that he'd left the area, at least temporarily. But, on November 1, I received a call from the U.S. Border Patrol in Blaine, to whom we routinely send lists of persons wanted either as witnesses or as perpetrators of crimes. The officer calling said, "We've a got a man in custody here who could be Douglas Ronald Anderson. We found that name in his effects but he has refused to say anything at all." "How tall's this man?" I asked. "Tallest son of a bitch I ever saw." came the reply. "Yes, that's Anderson. Did he give you any trouble?" "Well," said the officer, "I had to chase him. I chased him for about four blocks and had to tackle him in the end." "I've got a warrant for his arrest," I said "And I'll be glad to collect him, if you can take him to the Douglas crossing."

Constable Gotobed and I drove the 35 miles to the border in a wagon. On arrival, I could see Anderson in the back of a Border Patrol car with the cage shut; he was handcuffed and stretched out over the entire backseat. The patrolman who had caught him stood only about five foot eight, but he certainly looked tough enough to have done the job. He unlocked the rear door, and as we changed handcuffs, I identified myself and arrested Anderson on a charge of rape. "I'm an American citizen," he said, "I invoke the Fifth Amendment." The attending Canadian Immigration Officer now asked me, "Do you know where this man was born?" "Yes," I said, "Coronation, Alberta." "Is he a Canadian citizen?" "Yes, he certainly is." He then turned to Anderson and said, "I now declare you deported."

Gotobed and I then loaded Anderson and his three suitcases into our wagon and drove back to Vancouver. In his suitcases, I found a picture Anderson himself. And there was the Cowichan sweater with the skiers on it, exactly as described in the original report. This was crucial to our case, as Anderson would not admit that the luggage was his. As we exchanged his clothes, including his running shoes, for jail garb, he said, "Listen, Detective Welsh, this is only a game. It's only a match of wits between you and I." "Yes," I replied, "But if I lose, I don't do any time; if you lose, you'll do lots." Cross-checking, we found numerous reported offences for which Anderson appeared to be responsible. Various witnesses had described a man so tall that six foot four and a half Detective Davy, who usually accompanied me on these calls, was said to be short.

Routinely, we called for a line-up but now it became a problem. It was quite a job finding enough men of similar heights to display Anderson amongst. We resorted to going out on the street and found several very tall volunteers. When the time came, Anderson refused to participate at all, so I arranged a surreptitious line-up, with the witnesses behind one-way glass and instructed all the tall men to circulate around the room. I had to order Anderson to walk past the glass, because he knew what was going on. As he moved forward, he pulled his sweater over his face, but by that time, the witnesses had already identified him. But I kept everybody circulating for a while after that. This procedure went to court on two occasions and was ruled acceptable by both the County Court and the B.C. Supreme Court.

Anderson's brother visited me at the police station one day and said, "When you charge my brother as an habitual criminal, I would like to be a witness for the Crown." At the conclusion of his trail, Anderson was found guilty and sentenced to seven years for this rape and an additional six months consecutive for a street assault on a woman in whom he had tried to choke with her scarf. He was given an additional six years to run consecutively by Judge Swenziski in County Court on a charge of robbery. Since he had attempted to escape from the custody of Oakalla guards while he was being transported to one of these proceedings, he earned another year to serve. He came to public attention quite a bit after that. He was involved in a disturbance in the Pen, for which he received an additional sentence. He capped it all off by attempting to escape from the Pen; he hid inside the Pen under some loose floorboards for two days. Although the authorities thought that he had escaped, they did manage to locate him while he was still inside.

As is usual in most cases, I've never seen the young lady since; I do not know whether she returned to Germany or is still in the Vancouver area. The last I heard of her was when she phoned headquarters and inquired why two RCMP officers were about to pay her a visit. We sent two men to stake out her apartment and two RCMP officers did visit her. I think they had heard tales of her beauty and just wanted to meet her. The RCMP had no reason to visit her and were lucky that they weren't charged; perhaps they were disciplined by their superiors. All officers talk shop and we got to hear about a lot of crooks and their victims without being officially involved, but this is privileged knowledge and should never be used for the personal advantage of any officer.

It's not always a friendly neighbourhood, but sometimes our efforts to keep it nice are effective.

Thank God, I'm a Boy...

As night began to change into dawn on October 26, 1973, sixteen-year old Fred, who had been sleeping in his basement room, awoke with a start. The muzzle of his own .303 rifle wavered in front of his face. Blinking to focus his sleepy eyes, he realized that the person pointing it was wearing a nylon stocking mask. Sure that he had Fred's full attention, the masked man said, "I've never killed anyone before, have you?" "No, I haven't," replied the youth, "Have you?" His captor changed the subject: "I'm looking for valuables but you don't seem to have any." "Have you been upstairs?" Fred asked, wondering about his father, who slept on the main floor. "Yeah, but I didn't see anything worth taking."

The conversation strangely turned to other things and after a few minutes, when the intruder walked to the basement door, Fred went with him. At the door, the man took off the nylon mask, and Fred saw that he was a slightly built Black man in his twenties, standing about 5'10" to 6'0" tall, with a goatee and typical curly hair, and wearing blue jeans, a jean jacket and dirty work boots. They talked for a few more minutes and then the Black man handed Fred his rifle and left.

When Fred examined the rifle, he found that it was empty, just as he'd left it; obviously, the burglar hadn't found his ammunition stored in another part of the basement. Trembling with relief, he went upstairs and woke his father, who phoned in the breaking and entering report shortly before 6:00 am.

By the time PC McLellan arrived, Fred had found that $20.00 was missing from his jacket. He was lucky that he was not a female or he would probably have been raped.

I am impressed with the calmness with which Fred faced this situation, but it's hard to believe that an experienced criminal could be so stupid as to engage his victim in a lengthy conversation and finally remove his mask. It's strange, but it certainly helped us catch him in the end. We're lucky that most crooks really aren't very smart.

Burglars don't work regular hours and tend to be opportunistic criminals. So it wasn't surprising that he continued his prowl through the East End and struck again, only a few blocks away, around 8:00 am.

Nineteen-year old Carol, thinking that her dog was barking at the mailman or other animals that sometimes came around, checked her front door but found nothing. Ted, her live-in boyfriend, had left about an hour before to go to the Longshoreman's hiring hall to look for work. The dog, which was too small to frighten any intruder, was now barking at the rear door, and when she opened it and looked out, she saw a Black man standing with his back pressed against the house wall. As she tried to re-lock the door, he threw it open and came inside.

He had one hand in his jacket pocket and Carol thought he might have a knife or some other kind of weapon. She had a good look at him when she turned on the light. Apart from the blue jeans 'uniform,' Carol noted that he was wearing a dark floral button-down shirt and black platform shoes. (Fred probably mistook them for workboots) His hair was short on the sides and a little longer on the top but kinky and curly. His skin colour was medium to medium dark brown. She did not mention at this time whether or not he had a beard or mustache but he did in fact have a light goatee, a mustache and sideburns.

At this point, she decided that she was not going to resist. "What do you want?" she asked him. "Go to the bedroom," he replied. She was very frightened. He followed her in and closed the door, and she again asked "What do you want, what are you going to do with me?" He just smiled, while he looked around the room. "Are you going to rape or murder me or what?" she asked again and he said "I'm going to fuck you."

When he mounted her, he seemed to be having trouble maintaining an erection, as his penis kept slipping out of her vagina. On his third attempt, he managed to ejaculate, after which he got up and dressed. He had been attempting kiss her on the mouth and on her breasts during intercourse. "My only mistake is leaving you like this." he said and left.

Carol locked the doors and started to fill the bathtub to wash away the semen to avoid pregnancy. As she was about to get into the tub, her boyfriend came home and she told him what had happened. He called the police; PC Needham and RP Popil took the initial reports from Carol and Ted before driving them to Lions Gate Hospital where Carol was examined by her own doctor. When he examined her at 10:00 am, he was able to say that she had intercourse within the past 2 hours. While other hospitals may be closer, rape victims may have their private physician examine them in whichever hospital the doctor has visiting privileges.

Detectives Stanton and Stewart re-interviewed Carol and took written statements from her and her boyfriend later on October 26. They showed her the Morality mugshot book at this time but without any success. At this time, we had no suspect, but were convinced that the two crimes were committed by the same person.

Lohin and I were assigned this case when we reported for work that day. We showed both victims the mug book but they were unable to identify anybody in it. We issued a general description of the suspect to all police forces in the Lower Mainland and to every officer in Vancouver.

There had been several robberies in the East End whose suspect matched ours. One of these reports named a William Cathcart, said to be residing at Apartment 7, 1809 Commercial at the Victoria Diversion. When that report had been filed, the computer was down, so the usual check on his name had not been run. When the Major Crime Squad followed up on it, they found that there was no Apartment 7 and that no one there remembered seeing a Black man.

On November 3, 1973, PC Dolphin checked the accused at 2:40 am in the 1600 block Commercial Drive and noted that he fit the description circulated in connection with the above crimes but he did not run a CPIC (Canadian Police Information Centre) check on him as he received a radio call about a serious incident elsewhere that required his immediate attention and he left to attend to it. He did, however, submit a written report that he had checked him and that he seemed to fit the description we'd circulated.

Dolphin had noted that Cathcart had been very polite and cooperative; he had said that he certainly didn't feel he was being harassed just because he was Black. From his point of view, it might have been better if he'd kept his mouth shut, because he made too strong an impression on Dolphin. A CPIC check on Cathcart told us that his real name was Hannah, that although claimed that he was from Los Angeles, he had been born in Halifax, Nova Scotia. He was wanted in Toronto on a Canada-wide warrant for rape and breaking and entering, part of a series of 18 offences occurring between December 1972 and July 1973. The Immigration Department had also placed a hold on him. He was wanted by the Maricopa County Sheriff's Office in Phoenix, Arizona, on two counts of robbery and one of rape. He was not, by nature, a polite person.

At 10:30 am, on November 10, Nick and I went to 1809 Commercial, verified that there was no Apartment 7, and started knocking on all the apartment doors. Vancouver was not then the cosmopolitan mixture that it is now, and we felt certain that people would remember a Black man in the building. We thought he might just be an occasional visitor in the building. There was no resident caretaker, but the building was very neatly kept. Finally, we knocked on a second floor door and asked the lady who answered if there was a Black man in the building. She just pointed across the hall and shut her door in our faces.

Well, this was encouraging, so we radioed for assistance and shortly received four men in uniform. We used three of them to cover the exterior exits and approached the rear suite with the fourth man. Lohin's knock on the door brought no response. He knocked again and we heard stirrings inside. A woman's voice asked, "Who's there?" "Vancouver Police," said Lohin. She slid the bolt back but wouldn't open the door so Nick just pushed his way inside.

The place was sparsely furnished, and on a mattress on the bedroom floor, lay a naked Black man. Nick stepped into the room, pistol in hand, and said, "Are you Hannah?" He did not answer but just lay there; Nick stepped closer and waving his gun about two inches from his face, motioned for him to stand up, asking again, "Are you Hannah? "Yes, I'm

Hannah," he replied. We arrested him for rape and suspicion of rape and took him and the woman, who said she was Mrs. Hannah, downtown for further questioning and line-ups. From information on them supplied by the Toronto police, we were expecting to find a 'Mrs. Hannah,' or Susan Marie Hannah, aka Hann, who was also wanted in Toronto on a charge of soliciting and failing to appear for fingerprinting. Contrary to the popular misconception fostered by movies and television, fingerprinting is not always an automatic procedure in an arrest; frequently, the suspect is sent a notice to appear for fingerprinting at some later date. Failure to appear results in the issuance of an arrest warrant.

At 9:00 on November 7, Fred and Carol attended a line-up conducted by PC Mikita, at which they both positively identified Hannah. Carol said he was wearing the same clothes as he had on the day of the rape, with the exception of a different sweater.

We interviewed Hannah at 9:15 and advised him of the rape and breaking and entering investigations. He replied that he didn't commit either offence as he had only been in the city for a month; we knew that he'd been here for several months. When we told him that he had been identified as the rapist in the line-up, his only comment was, "I understand that." At 9:50, after consultation with Prosecutor K. Smith, we charged him with one count of rape, two of breaking and entering and one of theft.

When we notified the Maricopa Sheriff's Office that we had arrested William Eugene Hannah, alias William E. Cathcart, alias David A. Parker and charged him, the fun began. We also notified the police in Boston, Massachusetts, whom we now knew had an outstanding warrant for Hannah on a charge of forcible rape.

The Maricopa Sheriff replied promptly that he was sending an officer up to claim Hannah, who, on April 24, 1972, had broken into a motel room where he had raped and beaten a woman, breaking her nose, fracturing her skull and infecting her with a venereal disease. We advised him we had charges pending and could not release Hannah at this time but that he would be held for him at a future date.

Then the Toronto Metroploitan Police telexed us.

November 9, 1973

Chief of Police
City of Vancouver Police Department
Vancouver, BC
Attention; Det. R.M. Welsh
GIS Morality

Dear Sir:
Re: William Eugene Hannah
our MTP No. 6455/73
FPS No. 635652A
True Name William E. Cathcart
FBI No. 446 439 G

Confirming our exchange of telexes and CPIC messages of November 6, 1973, relative to the above named subject, this is to advise that this Department holds a Warrant for the arrest of Hannah aka Cathcart on a charge of rape. We also hold a Bench Warrant for his arrest on a charge of Breaking and Entering with an added charge of attempted Breaking and Entering.

This letter will confirm that we intend to return Hannah here for trial at the conclusion of your charges.

Between December, 1972, and July, 1973, a series of 18 offences were committed in the downtown Toronto area by a Black man who fits the general description of Hannah. All of these offences occurred within walking distance of Hannah's Toronto residence. All of these offences were either Breaking and Enterings, Assaults or Rapes.

We are aware that Hannah, whose true name is William E. Cathcart, is wanted in Phoenix, Arizona, under Phoenix Case No. 72-030280, where, under the alias of David Parker, he broke into a motel room on April 24, 1972, raped and beat a woman, breaking her nose and skull and infecting her with a venereal disease.

We would appreciate being advised of the circumstances surrounding Hannah's arrest and a brief synopsis of the offences he committed in Vancouver.

Please be assured of our co-operation in all matters of mutual interest.

Yours truly,

Bernard Simmons
Deputy Chief - Staff Operations

This letter prompted us to suggest to our Superintendent that the following letter should be sent in reply:

November 15, 1973

The Chief of Police
Metropolitan Toronto Police Department
590 Jarvis Street
Toronto, Ontario M4Y 2J5

Attention: Deputy Chief Bernard Simmons

Re: HANNAH, William Eugene, aka CATHCART

Dear Sir:

In reply to your letter dated November 9, 1973, we are forwarding a copy of our report to the City Prosecutor relating to our incidents. Enclosed are two photos of a line-up which was held for identification and which may assist you in your investigations of this subject.

It may be of further value to know that at the time of his arrest, HANNAH was accompanied by a white female, Susan Marie HANNAH, aka HANN, who was also arrested at the time and held for the Immigration Department. As a citizen of the United States, she has been deported there.

We have been in contact with the Sheriff's Office in Phoenix, Arizona, who wish to extradite the subject and also with Boston, Massachusetts, who also hold a warrant for rape for this person. They have been advised that he is being held here in preventive detention on our charges and that he will be held for your Department, when available, prior to being returned to the United States.

Please be assured that we will keep in contact and will advise you when Hannah will be available for escort.

Yours truly,

Detectives Welsh and Lohin

The Homicide and Robbery Division were also interested in this pair in connection with three taxi driver hold-ups in the recent past. None of the taxi drivers were able to identify either of the Hannahs in a line-up.

On May 10, 1974, in the midst of cross-examination during his trial, Hannah changed his plea from 'not guilty' to 'guilty.' Mr. Justice Fulton set June 4 as a sentencing date, and after court had adjourned, Hannah indicated that he would also plead guilty to another charge of breaking and entering at that time. In the event, sentencing was delayed until June 20, when Justice Fulton sentenced Hannah to 5 years and 6 months for rape and 2 years and 3 years to run consecutively on the two charges of breaking and entering.

In spite of his request that the Toronto charges be brought into B.C. and disposed of at that time, this wasn't done. Notwithstanding his guilty pleas, he then chose to appeal his sentences. His appeal was decided on February 27, 1975, when the sentences were reduced to 4 years and 6 months for the rape, and 2 years each on the two breaking and enterings, which were to be served concurrently with each other but consecutively to the rape sentence.

That was the last we ever heard of Hannah, so I can't say whether he was extradited to Toronto, Boston or Phoenix upon completion of his time in the Pen.

The Peanut Butter Rape

Late in the afternoon of October 7, 1969, PC Dowling visited a house in the 2400 block of Hemlock Street, where he spoke with a man who had phoned in a sexual assault complaint. This man, who played no further part in the case, told Dowling that four members of two motorcycle gangs, the local Coffin Cheaters, and Hell's Rebels from Winnipeg, had visited the house the evening before. They said they were looking for someone who had previously lived at the house and was involved in the drug trade. The man said he explained that he and his friends had recently rented the house and knew nothing about any previous tenants, and the motorcyclists left. At approximately 2:30 am, they returned. They stayed for a short while, during which one of them raped an under-age girl. When they left, they took an older girl with them to a party where she was raped by approximately ten gang members. Several items, including a stereo set, were also stolen during this visit.

The youngest victim, Debbie, who was thirteen years old at the time, said that she was in the front room when the gang members entered the house. A man she identified as Jerry came into the room and sat down beside her. He asked her to dance and she refused. After a minute or two, he asked her to give him a tour of the house, so she showed him through the various rooms. They came back into the front room and Debbie left to go to the bathroom. As she stepped out of the bathroom, she bumped right into Jerry, who had determined during the tour that there were no men in the house. Jerry grabbed her and pushed her back into the bathroom, forced her onto the floor, and started to undress her. He threatened to beat her up if she screamed or fought. He then had sexual relations with her. She was too afraid to scream or fight.

Afterwards, she went into the front room as the gang members left, and told her fifteen-year old sister Pat, "That guy raped me in the bathroom." The house on Hemlock was a hippie haunt with seven or eight youths living there. Both sisters had been told repeatedly by their mother and officers in the Youth Preventive Squad not to go there. They should have heeded good advice, but young people often don't.

Linda, who was eighteen years old, had left with one of the gang called Rogue, unaware that Debbie had just been casually raped in the bathroom. They had invited her to a party in a West End basement suite. She didn't know the address but was certain that she could locate the house if someone drove her through the area. The party consisted solely of members of the Coffin Cheaters and Hell's Rebels. She said she yielded to Rogue and had sexual intercourse with him, but when he had finished, he brought in nine or ten gang members who raped her while one of them held a razor at her throat. Finally, one of them called 'Mad John' had smeared her privates with peanut butter and got down and ate the peanut butter out of her privates. She said that he did this in front of all the other gang members.

Glen McDonald and I were assigned to this case. We soon got an address in the 700 block East 30th Avenue where some of these gang members were believed to hole up. Initially, we asked for a search warrant to try and locate the missing stolen goods, as we had learned from past experiences that it was awfully difficult to obtain suitable evidence to convince jurors of the validity of a rape claim in such circumstances.

We picked up PC Cliff Cooper, PC William Carlos and RCMP Constable Gray of the RCMP Motorcycle E Squad, drove into the East End.

I knocked on the door but there was no answer, so I sent two men around to the back door to see that nobody got out that way. I hit the door with my shoulder and went right in, leaping over people lying on the floor near the door. Cooper, who couldn't see past me, stepped on one of the bodies and it started screaming. Elsewhere, we found one man in bed with a Chinese girl. His head was shaven, leaving only a sizeable pony tail to compliment his beard. Although it was a small bedroom, there were several people in there. We arrested six gang members but released the two females.

We seized a motorcycle jacket with the letters 'FTW' on the back, which means 'Fuck The World,' and the word 'Chicklet' on one sleeve, as it matched the description that Linda had given us. We got one man in this group whose name was Jerry. We booked the six men under 'hold; investigation of rape.' We released a 22-year old motorcyclist from Renton, Washington, and told him to go home and stay home, though it was unlikely that he'd pay any serious attention to the warning. We recovered the stolen turntable and other stereo equipment at this house. Constables Cooper and Carlos later arrested another suspect named Michael at his address in Vancouver.

McDonald and I interviewed all the suspects. Some of them gave what were obviously bullshit lies about the alleged rape, while others stated that Linda was willing to have sex with them and to indulge in oral sex. They all denied threatening her with a razor. PC Jantzen conducted a line-up at 7:45 pm. At this time, Debbie was able to identify Jerry as the man who raped her on Hemlock Street and Linda was able to identify three persons out of this line-up. At the conclusion of the line-up, I took her into an interview room and said "You picked out three men ; could you tell me what these men did?" She said, "Number 10 is Rogue, the guy I went on the motorcycle with.; Number 14 is Jerry, who had sexual intercourse with me; and Number 7 is Mike, who also had sexual intercourse with me, while Rogue held my legs. I only saw three of them in this line-up."

At 8:25 pm., we held another line-up. Linda picked out numbers 15, 6 and 5. She said afterwards that, "Number 15 is 'Mad John' or 'Pony Tail,' the man who ate me out after filling my pussy with peanut butter; Number 6 was there but did nothing, he was asleep in the chair all the time; Number 5 is 'Chicklet,' who had sexual intercourse with me."

At 9:00 pm, we held a third line-up. Linda picked out numbers 3, 5, 7 and 9. She stated, Number 3 is 'Beard,' the one with the razor; Number 9 was 'Psycho,' They call him that because he's crazy; Number 7 was there but took no part. After the line-up, the people she did not identify were released. Jerry was charged with indecent assault on a female, sexual intercourse with a female under fourteen, rape, gross indecency, theft over $50.00, and possession of stolen property over $50.00. All the other gang members were charged with gross indecency, rape and indecent assault on a female.

On November 10, 1969, in the Provincial Court at 312 Main Street, a preliminary hearing was held for the eight motorcycle gang members. Constables Cooper and Carlos were assigned to help guard the prisoners, some of whom were still in custody. Those who had made bail now had on white shirts, suits and ties, and sported well-dressed short hair, in sharp contrast to their appearance when arrested. That alone must have been quite a shock to 'Mad John's' system, even though a month doesn't permit a normal head of hair to grow back in, they did look more 'civilized.' The suspects were scattered throughout the courtroom and I had to find and identify every one of them. I had anticipated this and I had made notes of moles, scars on their face, ring marks in their ears, etc., for each of them. All eight gang members were committed for trial by judge and jury in the high court.

In April 1970, the accused appeared at Assize Court at Vancouver, B.C. with Mr. Justice Aikins of the Supreme Court of British Columbia presiding. The proceedings ran for 22 days. McDonald and I were required to enter and give statements, then retire and then enter again to give evidence. When the gang members thought that we'd said something damaging to their defence, they would all get up and hiss, holler and catcall, carrying on something fierce. Judge Aikins was not amused and they came dangerously close to being declared in contempt of court on many occasions. While McDonald was giving evidence, he said that he didn't know anything about a broken door at the premises in the 700 block East 30th Avenue. When it was my turn to give evidence, the Defence Counsel asked me in cross-examination if I knew anything about breaking down the door. "Yes," I said, "I put my shoulder to it and broke the door down." Thinking that he had an advantage, he pursued the issue; "Why then," He demanded, "Didn't Detective McDonald know about this?" I couldn't see what the point was, but I answered, "Well, he wasn't there. I had sent him and one of the other officers to guard the rear of the house." I then noticed that Justice Aikins had a very pleased look on his face. But the Defence Counsel wasn't finished: "Did you know this was an issue in this court? Did you know that Detective McDonald has said that he did not know that the door of the house had been broken?" Now I was really puzzled. "No," I said, "Detective McDonald and I do not discuss our evidence while we're under cross-examination." This was, of course, true; any discussions we had felt to be necessary had been held much earlier! The motorcycle gang members were very edgy after this exchange. The whole issue of the broken door seemed to be meant only to confuse the jurors. It was immaterial; we had a search warrant and we had used no more force than was necessary to gain access to the house.

While in custody, one of the gang had managed to enjoy the sexual favours of a female 'friend' on the floor of in the women's washroom in the courthouse. This happened during one of the trial recesses. We found out when someone overheard the gang members bragging about it. I still can't figure out how he got away from the guard, who was a Sheriff's office employee, and not a police officer.

On March 6, 1970, the jury found all eight gang members not guilty of all charges. It is so very difficult to convince a jury that persons living an 'alternate lifestyle,' such as the hippies of that era or even prostitutes, can still be victims of crimes. Doubtless, the lack of adult supervision and seemingly loose morality of the victims must have swayed the jury, but I felt sorry for those two girls. I hope things improved for them afterwards. This was just another frustrating example of the very great difficulties all officers face in prosecuting sexual offences.

...Not the Hitchhiker's Guide...

The second half of November, 1969, found McDonald and I attached to the General Investigations Section of the Morality Squad, working the night shift from 6 pm to 2 am. At about 12:15 am, on November 19, we were cruising through the South Granville area in an unmarked car. McDonald was driving; he was probably the best high-speed auto chaser in B.C. He always kept the tank full of gas because he could – and would – outrun anybody and he'd chase them until they ran out of gas.

As we reached Fifteenth and Granville, heading south, we saw a black and white 1959 Ford proceeding west on Fifteenth from Hemlock turn into the north-bound lane of Granville at a high rate of speed. We made a U-turn and saw the Ford turn east on Fourteenth and right onto Hemlock Street. I radioed in our position, stating that we might be starting a chase, and asked for assistance. Up Hemlock Street, we followed them to Sixteenth and Granville where they made a sudden U-turn in the middle of the intersection, and accelerated east, turning right up the hill on McRae Avenue. McDonald was now in his element, and I was thankful for the new regulations regarding seatbelts! We now tore up McRae to the Crescent, a circular street about four-tenths of a mile around with a park inside and several streets radiating outward from it like the spokes of a wheel. I turned on the siren and the red light and unlatched my gun in its holster; there was no telling what these men had been up to and I wanted to be ready. We slid left at the intersection as the Ford pulled over to the inside curb, midway between McRae and Tecumseh Street.

I jumped out and ran up to the passenger's side with my gun drawn, but as soon as I got even with rear door, the driver floored it, and the chase was on again. I jumped back in, and we overtook it just before it reached Angus Drive, where they had meant to turn west and cross Granville. As McDonald pulled even with, them I pointed my gun at the driver's head and yelled, "Stop!" This time, he did it properly, and turned the key off. I noticed that the driver, whose name was Kelman, had his fly wide open. McDonald searched the passenger, Miller, and handcuffed him, asking him, "Why did you run from us?" Miller answered, "Some guy in a red car was chasing us. We thought you were him." The first patrol car to arrive and assist us held PCs Cooper and Caros, with whom we had just concluded a rape case. They could hardly believe it when they saw us there. We now searched the Ford and in the back seat we found a pair of ladies flowered silk panties, which were warm and dry. They seemed to have been worn very recently. We took Kelman and Miller to 312 Main Street, and prepared to investigate some type of complaint, but we sure as hell didn't know what kind as yet, other than the fact that they had committed several traffic violations.

Later that morning, we got a phone call from PC Cox, who had just taken a rape report from a young woman who had been hitchhiking earlier in the evening. The following material has been excerpted from Cox's report.

'At approximately 12:25 am, November 19,1969, a young man stopped me in the 700 block Granville. He said that he and his girlfriend were leaving a parking lot in the Kitsilano Beach area when they had heard a girl's cry for help. He had stopped and was walking up to a parked car when it started up and hurriedly left the parking lot. He got back into his car and followed it. Near the Planetarium, they met a young woman, mostly undressed, who was standing in the middle of the road. They understood immediately that she had been attacked, so his girlfriend helped her into the car. After hearing briefly what had happened, they began to follow the other car. They got close enough to identify it as a black and white 1959 Ford, 2 door sedan, B.C. licence 267-698. As they left Broadway and Cypress, the Ford managed to shake them off its tail. I then drove the victim, Jane, to Headquarters and took her statement.

'At approximately 11:30 that evening, she had been hitchhiking north on Kingsway at Commercial Drive when a car containing two men offered her a ride.

'She sat in the front between them; both men were of average build, in their early 20s and the driver had a mustache. They drove along Kingsway and west on Broadway. The conversation was of a general nature; they asked

Jane about her age, where she worked, etc. Now going north on Burrard, they turned west again just before the Burrard Bridge and then went north on Cypress to First Avenue.

'At this point, Jane became suspicious and asked to be let out of the car. She asked, "Where are you going?" The driver, whose name was Kelman, said, "We're just going down here for a minute." They moved north on Cypress, turned right onto Planetarium road, passed the Planetarium and parked in the parking lot by the beach. Kelman grabbed Jane and kissed her. She pulled away and tried to get out but Kelman put his arms around her. Miller, the passenger, tried to take off her slacks and while doing so ripped the zipper and right leg inseam down to the knee. Struggling against Miller, Jane reached across Kelman, opened his door and screamed, "Somebody help me!" Taken somewhat by surprise, Kelman closed the door and said, "If you don't stop yelling, I'm going to smash you!" By now Jane was on her back in the front seat and Miller had managed to remove her slacks and the leotards which she was wearing underneath. She was still wearing her panties. Miller then picked up the her legs and placed them over the back of the front seat and climbed into the backseat himself. Jane, attempting to stay in the front seat, grabbed the horn ring of the steering wheel and the horn sounded. Kelman grabbed her hands and pulled them roughly from the steering wheel. He heaved her bodily over the seat back towards Miller. Jane was still screaming and Miller shouted, "Shut up! Shut up!" He removed her panties and pulled his own trousers down to his knees, baring his penis. Jane managed to pull her knees tightly up towards her chest, so Miller had to wrestle with her in an attempt to have intercourse. He held both of her wrists in one of his hands and with the other was attempting to give himself an erection as well as placing his fingers in her vagina.

'After a couple of minutes of this unsuccessful action, Kelman said, "Let me try her." Jane did not believe that Miller had penetrated her with his penis; she thought that only his finger had actually made entry. Kelman either pulled down or removed his pants entirely while in the front seat before he climbed into the back and traded places with Miller. Kelman pulled Jane flatter onto the seat while

Miller held one of her legs over the back of the front seat, spreading her legs wide apart. Kelman climbed on top of her, and holding her hands, wrestled his way between her legs. He then began an up and down motion, lasting only two or three minutes. Jane said that he penetrated her vagina with his penis only as far as the head. She did not believe that he ejaculated, but could not say with certainty.

'Jane again managed to wind down the rear seat window and again screamed for help. A short time later, a young man appeared at the window. Kelman was still on top of her, having intercourse with her at this time. Miller, in the front seat, unnerved by the young man's appearance out of nowhere, started the car and drove out of the parking lot in a rush. As they were passing the Planetarium, Kelman jumped into the front seat and attempted to switch places with Miller. They couldn't do this without slowing to a crawl or stopping, and Jane jumped out of the car as it slowed down. She was standing in the middle of the road holding her torn slacks when the young and his girlfriend drove up and stopped.

'Jane was able to get the first three numbers of the licence plate, which were '267.' The young man was able to follow the car and completed the description when it stopped for the traffic lights at Broadway and Cypress. Shortly after this, realizing they had been followed, Kelman and Miller managed to shake them off. When they flagged me down, Jane was carrying green leotards and wearing three-quarter length brown coat over a brown pair of slacks. These slacks were ripped from the top of the zipper down the right leg to the knee. It was plain that she was not wearing any panties or underclothing. She said that the blue flowered bikini panties that she had been wearing were presently in the backseat of the Ford, along with her house key and possibly 50¢ in change. Jane had a small superficial cut on the left side of her lower lip. She said that the men did not attempt to remove her coat but just pushed it up.

'Jane was then taken to Vancouver General's Emergency Ward for examination. After a physical examination, the doctor said that the wet mount test was negative and that he would process the smear tests later in the morning. I then drove Jane to her home, where she quickly put on other clothes and gave me her torn slacks, both as evidence and for further testing.'

Spurred on by this coincidence, we began checking reports of recent rapes and found one whose suspects matched Miller and Kelman to a tee. Detectives Jack Cull and Duncan Cameron were the investigators. We provided them with line-up photos of our two suspects. As a result, the two hitchhikers, Clare and Louise, were shown the photos; Clare identified both men, who were charged with a further rape, but Louise was not absolutely certain in her identification. The following is an excerpt from the pre-trial report to the City Prosecutor.

'On the evening of Sunday, September 14, 1969, Clare and Louise, who were in their early twenties, were in the West End looking for an apartment. At approximately 11:00 pm, they were waiting at a bus stop on Granville Street between Davie and Nelson Streets, on their way home. Two men in a car pulled up alongside and offered them a ride, which they accepted. The men drove them to Louise's address on Cypress Street, where she got out. Clare, who was then working as a live-in housemaid, told the driver (Kelman) where she lived but a very short time after leaving Louise's place on Cypress Street, she realized that they were not driving her home. "Where are we going?" she asked, but Kelman said nothing and just kept driving. Clare said that at this time the passenger (Miller) appeared to be asleep but she now believes that he was pretending.

'They continued to drive and she repeatedly asked where they were going but neither of the men would answer. She began to feel very panicky. She remembers travelling along Southwest Marine Drive towards the University. Somewhere along there, Kelman pulled off the main roadway onto a dark road (Clare arrived from Scotland about two years ago; she doesn't drive and is unfamiliar with Vancouver, so she has been unable to identify the location) Kelman climbed into the backseat of the car and raped her – she screamed and fought but was overpowered. As Kelman and Miller were changing places, she rolled down the rear window and crawled part way out of it before

Miller dragged her back into the car by her legs, while Kelman rolled the window up against her so tightly that she though it was her last breath of air. They then drove her home and let her out of the car.

'At approximately midnight, Clare woke her employer, Mrs. Sullivan. Mrs. Sullivan opened her bedroom door and found Clare crying, "I'm sorry to bother you, but two men took me and raped me." Mrs. Sullivan saw that Clare was shaking badly, that her make-up had run and that her hair was in disarray. She attempted to calm Clare, who told her what had happened, who repeatedly interrupted her own story to say, "I thought they were going to kill me!" Clare was struggling then as she had in the car, to stay calm in order to save her life.

'Mrs. Sullivan took Clare to Vancouver General Hospital's Emergency Ward by taxi, where she was examined at approximately 1:35 am. The general examination revealed numerous dirt streaks on her hands, face and arms, some bruising and tenderness of the rib cage and a short but pronounced scrape on the outside of her right thigh.

'The pelvic examination confirmed that she had been raped. Smears taken at the time showed the presence of a moderate number of active sperm within the vagina.

'The doctor gave Clare a mild sedative, as she was very agitated and was still trembling in occasional spasms. He emphasized that she should consult her own doctor first thing in the morning.

'PC Law interviewed Louise, who confirmed the details of Clare's story up to the time she was dropped off at her Cypress Street address but was unable to describe the suspects.

'Detectives Cull and Cameron visited Clare at 7:45 am on the morning of November 21, 1969, and showed her a police line-up photo containing ten men: she immediately pointed out Kelman and Miller as the men who had raped her on September 14, 1969. They also showed her a pair of dice, a rubber animal, badges and an animal tail, which she immediately identified as articles that she had seen in the rapist's car and had subsequently described to the police.

'When Louise was shown the line-up photo, she was unable to identify the suspects, but she was certain that the rubber animal and the dice were similar to those she had observed in the car on September 14. For the record, these items had been removed from Kelman's car in the Police Garage for the purpose of displaying them to the victims and witnesses.'

At 10:50 am, on November 21, Detectives Cull and Cameron arrested Miller, who was out on $2500.00 bail, at his Vancouver address. They identified themselves and advised Miller of the nature of our investigation and warned him but he had nothing to say

At 11:50 am, Nick and I arrived at Oakalla to interview Kelman, who had been returned to custody after we arrested him that night on the Crescent, for violating his parole from two 2-year sentences he had been serving concurrently since September 9, 1968, for indecent assault. He had been paroled on July 17, 1968. We again identified ourselves, advised him of the nature of the charge and warned him in the standard manner:

Q: Do you understand?
A: Yes.
Q: Wish to say anything?
A: No.
Q: Is that your '59 Ford, licence 267-698, which is being held in the Police Garage?
A: Yes.
Q: Are you the registered owner.?
A: Yes
Q: Do you wish to release it to someone?
A: Yes.
Q: You will need to give someone a slip of paper authorizing the release of it to them.
A: Okay, I have someone coming in to visit me today.

Finally, at 1:00 pm that day, we consulted with the Assistant Prosecutor, Mr. Bendrodt, who instructed us to charge them both with two counts of rape.

Both victims, Jane and Louise, were shown Kelman's car on Sunday evening before it was released. They both identified it as the car used in their rapes.

The preliminary hearing was held on December 22, 1969, before Provincial Court Judge Bernard Isman. During cross-examination, the Defence Counsel asked why I had then pulled a gun on the two accused. I said, "In circumstances similar to this, I would again pull a gun. I did not know what these two men had been responsible for, whether they'd just committed a robbery or what. I feared for my life; I felt they were very dangerous." Judge Isman took up this line of questioning himself: "For those two reasons you would draw a gun on a person?" "Yes, sir," I said. Judge Isman agreed with the Defence Counsel, saying, " It was very wrong of you, Detective Welsh, to pull this weapon on these two men," and further chastised me, saying, "You would do this again?" Annoyed, I said, "I am under oath. I have told you I that I drew my gun and I would do it again." Eleven years later (1980), I was still on the police force and Judge Isman was long gone from the Bench. But he did, in fact, commit both Kelman and Miller for high court trial.

And on May 7, 1970, in Assize Court, for the rape of Louise, the housemaid, Kelman was sentenced to six years plus the unexpired portion of his sentence outstanding from September 9, 1968, thus adding 398 days to his total. On October 30, 1970, in the matter of the assault on Jane, the charge was reduced to indecent assault on a female and he received 4 years to be served concurrently with the sentence imposed on May 7. On March 4, 1971, the appeal against the conviction of May 7, 1970, was dismissed. At the Crown's request, in the Supreme Court of British Columbia, on June 1, 1971, he was declared a dangerous sexual offender, and was sentenced to preventive detention in lieu of the four years imposed on October 30, 1970, He appealed the sentence of May 7, 1970, but on October 26, 1971, this appeal was refused as abandoned. Miller got off quite a bit lighter, as he appeared to be more of a 'follower,' although he did receive a substantial sentence in the Penitentiary.

The coincidences were rather remarkable. We had just finished a long rape case and came out onto the street, only to arrest two persons in a speeding car to find that they had just committed a rape. The coincidental arrival of PCs Cooper and Caros as next on the scene to assist us added to the effect. Perhaps it isn't as strange as it may seem, since I used to try to get Cooper, who was a big and tough, and had been a cowboy on the Prairies prior to becoming a policeman, whenever I thought I needed some extra muscle, and I'm not a small man myself. His partner, Bill Caros had a classic Greek physique and was quite an athlete. Two damned good men to have on our team. Both of these officers have since retired. At the time of writing, (1980) Detective McDonald was still on the Force and still drove the same way. Christ, he could have qualified at the Indianapolis Speedway. The end result of what I thought was great police work, in which we'd gone beyond the call of duty, was that we didn't even get a thank you. At that time, all the old Inspectors and Staff Sergeants said, "That's what the Hell you get paid for."

Unhappy Reunion

In August of 1973, Kate, who had been living in Winnipeg for some years, flew home to Vancouver for a visit. On August 10, she and her brother Will decided to go to one of the downtown cabarets for drinks and some dancing. They arrived about 9:45 and in the course of the next few hours, they had several drinks and fell into friendly conversation with a young man named Ken who had gradually made his way to their table. Kate felt good but not intoxicated, but her brother Will was a heavier drinker and he was becoming drunk. Kate had a few dances with Ken and after the cabaret closed, the three of them went to an all-night pizza parlour. Ken picked up the tab and offered to give them a ride home, even though their parent's apartment was only a few blocks away in the West End.

They walked from the pizza place to the lane behind the cabaret where Ken's car, a white Ford, was parked. Kate got into the front seat, moving toward the middle to make room Will, but Ken suddenly drove away, leaving Will standing in the lane.

Kate began to scream and thought about leaping from the car, and kicked at the door twice trying to open it, but she was belted in and was afraid of being run over if she merely fell out on the street. She continued to scream and Ken lunged at her, catching her by the throat and making the car swerve alarmingly. "Shut up!" he said, "Will told me to take you and get us some more beer. But first, we're going to a friend of mine's and then we'll pick up Will." Kate stopped screaming and trying break out of his tight grip on her throat. She could not slip out of his grip, and as she calmed down and quit trying, he relaxed and finally released his hold on her.

Still very frightened, Kate began to recognize some landmarks. She didn't know how long they had been driving but she realized, as they passed the PNE, that they were driving east on Hastings Street. A short time later, Ken turned left, went up a slight hill and drove quite a ways down the other side into a narrow paved road, which was closely shrouded by bushes on both sides.

When he stopped, the lights of the PNE were clearly visible to the west; towards the north was a large body of water, obviously Burrard Inlet, but Kate could not see either the Second Narrows bridge nor the low-level railway bridge.

Ken had parked Kate's side of the car tight against the bush, and he now dragged her bodily out of the car, saying "If you don't co-operate, I'll kill you. A girl was killed here a week ago."

Kate asked, "Did you kill her?"

Ken made no reply but just smiled and began pulling Kate's jeans down. He ripped her panties, and left them hanging around her ankles. He shoved her down onto the ground and raped her. More afraid for her life now than she had been before, Kate submitted. Shortly, Ken stood up, and allowed Kate to stand and pull her pants up. He said that he had this hang-up and that he treated all the girls he went out with this way. From that point on, Ken repeatedly said he was sorry, as if that could correct the situation. He claimed that it was his wife's fault; she had left him while he was serving two years in jail, and was now living with another man.

Kate told him that he needed a psychiatrist and he agreed that he probably did. He offered her money or anything else that she wanted but she just wanted to go home.

Kate was now in a state of shock and soon found herself in the car heading back past the PNE. After driving her slowly around Stanley Park, which made Kate think that he was going to attack her again, Ken dropped her off in the West End near her parent's apartment at about 5:30 am. He pointed across the water towards the Kitsilano Beach area and said, "That's where I live." and drove off. Kate, frightened and confused, was unable to recall anything useful about Ken's car. Kate then woke her parents and told them of the rape.

When PC Doern and acting Cpl. Mason interviewed Kate between 2:30 and 5:30 pm on August 11, she told them that her mother had destroyed her panties and jeans and had insisted upon her having a bath after she had told her of the rape. Kate was fortunate to have sustained only minor physical injuries during the attack. Doern and Mason decided that an examination by a doctor was unnecessary, as it would have proven nothing at that stage.

Doern asked Kate why she didn't report the rape as soon as she arrived home. She said that she was too upset at that time to talk to the police. Mason interviewed her parents, who confirmed that Kate had arrived home around 5:30 am; she had been very hysterical and kept repeating that she had been raped.

Her parents said that their son Will arrived at approximately 8:00 am, saying that he had too much to drink the night before and had spent the night in a hotel. He was unaware of Kate's circumstances until then, but he told them that he could positively identify Ken and that Ken was a well-known patron of that cabaret. Doern and Mason were unable to interview Will as he had left for Fort St. John at 11:30 that morning, where he was employed by Bouchard Construction; he would not be home again for four months.

At the time of this interview, Kate was still visibly upset. Doern and Mason told her and her parents to expect a visit from Morality Squad detectives within the next day or two, probably on August 13.

On the morning of August 12, 1973, Nick and I interviewed Kate at her parent's apartment and took a written statement from her. We showed her photos of Morality suspects but she was unable to identify any of them. We made arrangements for a police artist to visit her and make a composite sketch of the suspect. On August 14, after the sketch was done, Kate returned home to Winnipeg. She was very concerned about what her husband would say if he found out what had happened. Obviously, she wasn't going to tell him; that was their problem.

Joe Stanton and Ken Stewart did the follow-up on the night shift; they visited the cabaret and discovered that one of the waitresses was a policeman's daughter. She was very helpful and recognized the man in the sketch right away, saying, "If that's the man, I know him as Ken, but his beard is a little too full in the sketch. He's often in here." So Will had been correct. She agreed to phone the police the minute he showed up. With only the sketch and the incomplete car description, there was nothing else to do but wait and hope.

On the evening of August 31, PCs Edgar and Carpenter visited the cabaret in response to the waitress' phone call and subsequently arrested the suspect, whose real name was Kenneth Wayne Gillespie. He was held without charge pending the investigation of a rape.

PC Awcock ran a very unusual line-up for us on the same day. Since Kate could not be present, as she was back in Winnipeg, we photographed the line-up and sent a copy to Winnipeg with photographs of two other line-ups. The Winnipeg Police told Kate that if she saw the man who raped her in any of the photos, she was to put her name and the current date on the back of the photo and they would return it to the Vancouver City Police. She studied the photos carefully and, on the third photo, she positively identified our suspect. The next day, all we could get out Gillespie was that he sometimes went to that cabaret and that he vaguely remembered meeting a man and a woman there but he could not remember what day it was. We did establish that he was then a parolee, that he had three years of parole to serve and that his parole officer was either a Mr. McGougan on Nanaimo Street or a Mr. Zillman on East Hastings, neither of which turned out to correct.

On June 20, 1967, Gillespie had been sentenced to two years less one day definite and one year indefinite for robbery with violence in Nanaimo. By December 10, 1968, he had already been paroled for the first time. For criminal negligence in the operation of a motor vehicle, he served fourteen days, paid a $500 fine, received a three months indefinite sentence and was prohibited from driving in Canada for two years on July 17, 1970. He was convicted of attempted rape on February 14, 1972, and sentenced to two years less one day and was required to serve three years probation upon release. Release was again amazingly prompt; he was paroled for the second time on December

29, 1972, after serving approximately twenty-eight months of his accumulated minimum of four years. We charged him with rape and released him on bail.

We found later that his parole officer was a Mr. Sadler in Victoria; on July 24, he had raped a woman in the Nanaimo area and had been committed for trial there on August 21. Having raped Kate in the meantime, he did not show up for his Nanaimo court appearance and there was a warrant for his arrest on that charge as well.

On September 13, when Nick and I went to pick up Gillespie at his job as an auto body repairman on Seymour Street, we were told that he had quit at the end of the previous week and that they believed that he might have moved to Duncan. We issued a warrant for his arrest and notified the RCMP in Duncan. On September 17, PC Davis collected Gillespie from the Duncan RCMP and returned him to Vancouver.

Gillespie was tried in Provincial Court by Judge Biernes in the first instance of a trial by judge for the crimes of rape or murder. Previously, the law required that a preliminary hearing be held in lower court and the accused could elect to be tried either by a judge and jury or by a judge alone, but a recent change in the Criminal Code of Canada permitted prosecutors to ask for a direct indictment to the higher court.

The defence counsel was Chester Bridle, who had previously been a Crown prosecutor; Nick and I knew him quite well. Bridle was insistent that his client was innocent and that we were trying to railroad him. He claimed that Gillespie couldn't have been responsible as he was in Nanaimo at the time of the offence. Bridle said that Gillespie had taken the last ferry of the night and had arrived after his parents were asleep; he quietly let himself in and went to sleep on the couch, where they found him the next morning. Supporting witnesses were brought from Nanaimo, including the accused's parents, but since he could only produce a ferry ticket stub from Nanaimo to Horseshoe Bay, dated August 11, we weren't too concerned about this fabrication. Without a Horseshoe Bay to Nanaimo ferry stub dated August 10, this defence was ridiculous. We were convinced that, after raping Kate, he had driven to Horseshoe Bay and caught the first morning ferry to Nanaimo in order to establish his alibi.

One unusual aspect of this trial was that Kate's brother Will, who was drunk at the time of the incident, had originally claimed that he could identify Ken, but he was later unable to pick him out of a very good line-up photo on September 12. However, when the suspect was hidden in the courtroom, Will went around to look at everyone and he picked him out without any trouble whatsoever. He said later that "...bells just began to ring as I approached him." Kate did not testify in person at the trial, but her evidence was presented in the form of a sworn statement.

Judge Biernes found Gillespie guilty as charged. Counsel Bridle had a veritable fit and asked Judge Biernes for his reasons for judgment. Judge Biernes refused him, rapped his gavel and said, "Four years in the Penitentiary. Case closed."

Chester Bridle appealed the conviction and on January 18, 1974, Gillespie was granted a new trial. He was committed for re-trial by a judge and jury on November 13, 1974. In the meantime, we had gathered further evidence indicating that his parents may have been mistaken about their son's presence in Nanaimo during the night of August 10-11; consequently, they weren't called as witnesses for the new trial. This time, Kate appeared and testified. On February 26, 1975, Gillespie was found guilty of rape and was sentenced to six years.

It is ironic that one of his victims could tell Gillespie that he needed a psychiatrist, and that he would agree with her. It seems that no one else in the corrections system had enough sense to protect the public by insisting that he be given psychiatric counselling. Kate wishes to hell that someone had done it earlier.

Progress to Murder

On October 26, 1969, Lohin and I were working the Morality Detail on the 6 pm to 2 am shift. We received a radio call to assist in the investigation of a rape which had occurred in Renfrew Park. PC Flynn was still on the scene but the 15-year old victim had already been sent to the hospital for examination. We carefully inspected the cordoned-off scene but were unable to come up with anything. A general search of the neighbourhood and a police broadcast describing the attack produced nothing.

Ruth, who was 15 years old at the time, had been visiting relatives in Richmond and, at 8:30 pm, was returning to her home near 21st Avenue and Nootka Street, close to Renfrew Park, when she was accosted. This area is very well lit; there is a strong street light right above the attack site and so Ruth got a good look at her attacker. She was forced to undress at knife point and was assaulted.

Nick and I caught up with Ruth at the hospital and got a full statement from her at that time. It was noted that she had minor bruises on her face and head. She says she was raped although Dr. Brammell, the City Pathologist, said that he did not believe that penetration was made due to the fact that she was very small, although sperm were found around the external genitalia. Later, PC McLarty interviewed Ruth and prepared a composite drawing of the suspect.

With no witnesses or suspects, the investigation quickly ground to a halt. This is very common and all policemen learn to be patient but the best learn never to forget; Ruth didn't either. In the first week of April, 1970, she called us; she believed that she had seen her attacker at Rollerland at the PNE. On a second occasion, she obtained the licence number of his Honda motorcycle, which led us to Douglas Robert McCallum, 23 years of age, and a resident of East Vancouver. On April 9, 1970, we interviewed McCallum, who bore a striking resemblance to the composite drawing made up to match Ruth's description. McCallum appeared to be mentally handicapped to some degree. I asked him if he knew anything about a rape last Hallowe'en. "When's Hallowe'en?" he asked. "You know," I said, "In the fall–

with firecrackers and trick or treating–that stuff." "I don't know anything about it," he said. "What–Hallowe'en?" I asked. "No," he replied, "that rape." He did, however, readily consent to take part in a line-up. At PC Tyler's line-up, Ruth identified him without any hesitation; she swore that he was the rapist.

I consulted Det. Stevenson on the merit of a polygraph or lie detector test in these circumstances and we agreed to ask McCallum to submit to one. Again, McCallum was very co-operative. When Stevenson arrived, McCallum asked, "Is a polygraph test a blood test?" Stevenson looked at me quizzically and I told McCallum, "No, it's a lie detector test." Still uncertain, McCallum asked, "Is that where they stick something up your ass?" Stevenson tested him for approximately 1 hour and 25 minutes.

In conclusion, he was unable to determine anything at all about McCallum. He had met many liars who were guilty and probably some innocents who felt guilty but he'd never met anyone who was so enigmatic as McCallum. He neither appeared to be concealing anything nor overly concerned about being suspected of a crime. Some of his responses to non-threatening questions seemed to be excessively complicated but his physiological responses were rather unvaried. Stevenson believed that he was suffering from some sort of congenital defect or mental illness. He did not appear to know the meaning of rape, nor did he know what he was doing last week. At one point, he said that he did not rape a woman last October but he couldn't even tell how far he'd gone in school other than that he was in special classes.

Mental incompetence is a powerful defence, when it is genuine; the suspect seemed to match Ruth's description but had no priors of any sort, so we discussed the case with Prosecutor Bendrodt. He and I met with Ruth and her mother on April 11, 1970. As a result of this interview, the prosecutor laid a charge of rape against McCallum.

At the preliminary hearing, the accused was committed for trial by judge and jury, and was subsequently convicted of attempted rape. He got a three-year suspended sentence. Everybody went about their lives again.

On June 13, 1973, at 11:45 pm, a man who lived in the Broadway and Renfrew area was out with his dog, waiting at a bus stop for his wife to return from work, when he heard a series of what he thought were firecracker explosions, three bangs in a row, then a fourth. With time to spare, he walked in the direction of the noises and in the 2800 block East Fourteenth, he found a woman lying face down partially on the sidewalk with her head in a driveway. He ran to the nearest telephone but it was out of order. He managed to stop a passing police motorcycle officer, Cpl. R. Davies, who immediately radioed for assistance. The victim, Geraldine Forster, was despatched by ambulance to Vancouver General's Emergency Ward, where she was pronounced dead on arrival.

Geraldine had walked a visiting friend approximately five blocks to a bus stop on Broadway, and was walking home when slain. Nothing in her life pointed to any possible cause for murder. Dr. Brammell's autopsy the next morning yielded only two copper jacketed lead bullets; the other two had apparently missed the victim. A thorough search of the crime scene, which had been cordoned off overnight, produced only one .38 calibre shell casing.

On June 14, while he was preparing for duty, Constable Dingle of the Sechelt RCMP Detachment found that his Sam Browne belt, his .38 calibre Smith & Wesson revolver and twenty rounds of ammunition were missing from his closet. He had last seen them at approximately 1 am on June 11, when he returned to his home on Tyson Road, three miles south of Sechelt. It was his standard procedure to put the belt, the revolver and its holster and the ammunition pouch in the bedroom closet at the end of each work day. On June 11, he did that and then went on his usual three-day weekly leave; sometime during this interval, the gun had been stolen. He immediately reported his loss and the investigation fell to Sgt. W. Saunders of the local RCMP, who found no point of forced entry, but a window in an adjacent bedroom was found to be closed but unlocked; yes, policemen sometimes make mistakes, too.

Weapons thefts always get wide reportage within the police community, especially when a policeman is the victim, and as soon as we learned of Dingle's loss on June 16, we wondered whether his gun had been used in the puzzling murder on East Fourteenth. Constable Dingle had previously been a member of the Powell River Detachment and, in the course of his tour there, had fired numerous rounds of target practice. Curious as it might seem, neither manufacturers, who test-fire all weapons before shipment, nor police forces keep sample bullets from their own weapons; part of it is just logistics and economy but part of it relates to the superstitious dislike of preparing for the possible loss of the weapon. In sports psychology, once you can get your opponent to start preparing for a loss, some people feel that makes the loss more likely to occur. So Sergeant Andrews and Detective Cameron spent June 17th at the Powell River RCMP range and returned with one and a half cartons of spent shell casings.

After much time-consuming work, Jeff Hilton of the Crime Lab made 120 positive comparisons between spent Powell River shells and the spent shell found at the murder scene. Jeff also test-fired all RCMP weapons known to have been fired at the Powell River range by other RCMP officers during Dingle's tour of duty without finding any positive matches; Dingle's gun was the murder weapon. While bullets may deform to the point of being impossible to compare, shell casings are generally hardy, and identifications can be made on the basis of firing pin imprints and extractor/ejector markings.

On June 21, 1973, a resident of the Sechelt area turned over to Sergeant Saunders a Sam Browne belt and holster which he had found on June 13 at 4:20 pm, approximately 300 yards north of Tyson Road and Highway 101. The Sam Browne belt and holster were lying in plain view alongside the highway. The man had been driving a backhoe loader at the time and did not turn the items in until he saw the theft reported in the local newspaper. At this point, the trail faded; in the months immediately following, suspects were checked out across B.C., parts of Alberta and the Northwest Territories, all to no avail. In spite of the many hours which were spent on it in Sechelt and Vancouver, nothing further turned up and the case was superseded by more urgent matters that always fill each police day.

At 1:10 am, on April 30, 1976, three years after the murder, PCs Boutine and Needham were checking the premises in the 300-block of West 5th Avenue. At one location, they found the fire escape door had been jimmied, but there were no intruders inside. Luckily, they spotted and stopped a man walking east in the lane behind the building. It was Douglas McCallum. As the result of questioning, he led them to his truck, and it was searched by Boutine. Hidden in the springs under the seat, Boutine found Constable Dingle's stolen revolver, fully loaded.

Continuing his search, Boutine then found a brown leather pouch containing ten live rounds of ammunition. It should be noted that the gun did not show any signs of rust nor did the pouch show any signs of mould, as they would have if they had been kept in the truck for some length of time; this implied that they had been stored properly elsewhere and had been put there for some specific and immediate purpose. Also under the front seat were a 9-inch knife, a starting pistol, some surgical gloves, a road map, three other green gloves and two cigarette packages with licence numbers written on them. Boutine warned McCallum regarding the stolen revolver. "I found that gun on Rupert Street about a month ago, " McCallum replied. McCallum was then formally arrested. A copy of the police report attached to the file was sent to the Homicide and Robbery Squad. McCallum's story began to weaken when he was warned about the possible consequences of possessing the gun, and he than claimed to have found the weapon in a paper bag the morning before (which would have been April 29, 1976) at 12th and Rupert Street; he said noticed the barrel of the gun sticking out of the bag.

With this gun in hand, Jeff Hilton made a positive comparison to the firing pin imprint on a cartridge found at the murder scene. The barrel's rifling was badly pitted since it had not been cleaned regularly and Hilton could not make a completely positive identification of the bullets taken from Geraldine Forster until May 6, 1976, when he test-fired the revolver in double-action mode.

On April 30, 1976, at 6:35 pm, Detectives Cameron and Cliffe interviewed McCallum, who claimed that he was looking for lampshades in dumpster bins when he was arrested and that he was en route to the police station with the gun which he'd found on Rupert Street behind the RCA Victor TV premises, while he was going to work at Panco Poultry. He said that he stopped his truck because there was a fire by a sign, and that he found the gun on the grass with the leather shell pouch. He took the gun and, after hiding it under the front seat of his truck, he went to work. Almost casually, someone asked McCallum if he travelled much. "No," he replied, "But I've been to Osoyoos and I was on the Sunshine Coast about 3 years ago, with a friend of my father's." Cameron and Cliffe looked at each, trying not to betray their feelings of satisfaction; it now seemed possible that McCallum might have stolen the gun and used it to kill Geraldine Forster.

His father's friend, Sam Moore, was interviewed and recalled taking McCallum to Sechelt. And even that he'd taken him to the Dingle residence in June of 1973. Moore's wife owned the house and he had McCallum help him to replace some damaged ceiling tiles in one of the rooms. Dingle omitted the ceiling tile replacement from his loss report because it occurred while he was at work; but his girlfriend, who should have mentioned it to him, recognized McCallum's photo when she was shown it in 1976.

In the course of the investigation, McCallum had been interviewed several times by different officers. He had changed his story about finding the gun and had given us vague statements about his time on the Sunshine Coast; he claimed to be unable to describe any part of the towns he had passed through. He could not recall paying income tax and said that he had a problem reading, writing and remembering, although his driver's licence indicated that he had a reasonable competency at those tasks.

Other holes began to appear when he said that he had been employed by Western Canada Steel for six years, until he quit in October 1975; at the time of the rape in 1969, he claimed to be employed by a North Van trucking company. He had, in fact, been fired by from two of the three jobs he'd held since 1972. He had started at the steel company in late April of 1972 and had been fired in mid-October of 1975 for various locker room thefts – charges were not pressed. But the Company had been on strike from March 1973 to July 1973, giving him ample opportunity to visit Sechelt.

With information supplied by Sam Moore, we learned that McCallum had worked as a chokerman for a logging company in nearby Port Mellon on June 6, 7, 8 and 11, 1973. Their payroll records confirmed this. Now followed a series of visits to the Sunshine Coast where witnesses were found who placed McCallum in Sechelt on June 13, 1973. One person had written out and given cheques to Moore while another recognized McCallum's photo and said that he was present when Moore received those cheques.

At 1:30 pm, on May 7, 1976, Douglas McCallum was served with a warrant for non-capital murder. When he was charged, he characteristically said nothing at all.

As for motive, none ever really emerged. McCallum would not, or more likely, could not adequately explain his own motives for doing many things. Poor Geraldine Forster just happened along at the wrong time. McCallum never admitted his guilt, although there was no doubt in our my minds that he was cleverer in some respects than he claimed to be; we believed that he knew which of his acts were morally and legally wrong.

So did a judge and jury. The Assize Court of British Columbia convicted Douglas McCallum of non-capital murder and sentenced him to life imprisonment.

No Remorse

In the summer of 1971, two bizarre events occurred.

Although it was relatively rare in those days, the Burnaby RCMP had a breaking and entering in which a young white male had robbed a couple at knife-point before kidnapping the wife. Clear of the house, the man had evaded all roadblocks and drove to the Squamish area, approximately 50 miles north of Vancouver, where he repeatedly raped the woman, threatening her again and again with the knife. Two days later, he released her in Vancouver. The woman had been so traumatized that, in spite of spending two awful days with him, she could give only the most general description of her rapist.

On the way back, her kidnapper had stopped at a motel and bought cigarettes, but she had been unable to get out of the car. She couldn't remember the name or even the location of the motel so the RCMP checked every motel from North Vancouver through Horseshoe Bay up to Squamish. They found a motel whose owner remembered a car entering the motel driveway and a man coming in to buy cigarettes. He said, "I wrote the licence number down on a piece of paper." he said, "I do that on any occasion when a car enters my motel late at night. Since the man caused no trouble, I threw the piece of paper in the garbage. It's in a barrel out back, waiting for pick-up." The RCMP went through the barrel, scrap by smelly scrap, but they recovered the paper with the licence number on it; he had been the only suspicious night visitor for several days.

I was working in the General Investigation Section of the Morality Squad at the time and received a call on August 17 from the RCMP, who gave me the licence number, in the hope that we might just stumble upon the car in the course of daily work. The car, which had been stolen several days earlier, was still on our list. I made note of the licence number and the description of the suspect for the Information Bulletin and sent a copy to the police radio, including the suspect's involvement in the North Burnaby kidnapping. Within seconds, Constable Bob Gemmell radioed in, "That car is in front of me on Hastings Street being driven by a white male with red hair." Gemmell and his partner pulled the vehicle over without incident and arrested a man who gave his name as Robert Allan Street. Gemmell instantly noticed that the red hair was a dye job: the darker roots were starting to grow out. Street was charged with possession of stolen property, the automobile, and was fingerprinted as a matter of course. We were surprised when the prints were identified as those of Glen Wayne Jansen, aged 21, who had escaped from the Pen on July 23. We laid an additional charge of escaping lawful custody against him and turned him over to the Burnaby RCMP, who charged him with robbery, rape and kidnapping.

On October 13, 1971, he was convicted on the charges of possession of stolen property and escaping lawful custody, and was given 6 months on each count to be served consecutively with the remainder of his previous sentence, which had been 15 months definite and indefinite for breaking and entering with intent to commit a crime of which only 9 months had been served. On June 8, the rape charge arising from the abduction of the Burnaby woman was dropped, but on June 13, 1972, in the Supreme Court of BC in New Westminster, he was convicted of robbery and kidnapping, and sentenced to seven years on each count, to be served concurrently.

Jansen first entered the system on November 3, 1967, when, at the age of sixteen, he was transferred from Children's Court to face three counts of breaking and entering and one count of indecent assault. He received 12 moths definite and 36 months indefinite on these charges and was paroled by January 23, 1969.

Barely two months later, his parole was revoked and he drew an additional 6 months for possession of a stolen car. Stealing cars interested him more than working to buy one, so on October 7, 1970, he was in trouble again, violating his parole of July 24 and earning 2 years less a day, both definite and indefinite. After a lengthy appeal, these were reduced to fifteen months each on May 21, 1971. In the meantime, he had been recommitted on February 11 as a parole violator. He didn't take kindly to prison and escaped on July 23, 1971. On August 17, Gemmell arrested him on Hastings.

On October 28, 1974, he was released on day parole to the Burrard Centre, in the YMCA in downtown Vancouver, in spite of being sentenced to lengthy terms in 1972. Jansen found work with the City, planting trees in the West End in one of a number of beautification programs.

At this time, Vancouver Police were not aware that these types of criminals were being paroled so early and so easily. Since then, steps have been taken to correct this situation, but as noted earlier, the parole system is full of loopholes and there is no legal requirement at present to notify any police force that so-and-so, with a record of such-and-such, has been paroled in your area.

In the spring of 1975, a series of indecent assaults and robberies in the Downtown area began puzzling police. On March 31 at 8:00 pm, a 24-year old woman was attacked in an underground parking lot in the 1000 block Haro Street; On April 10, at 6:00 pm, a 45-year old woman was victimized in the same parking lot; on April 18, in the 100 block West Pender, a 37-year old woman reported a similar attack; shortly after noon on May 21, a 42-year old woman was indecently assaulted in the Hudson's Bay Company parkade at Georgia and Seymour, and finally, in late June, the pattern changed abruptly.

In response to a call from the lot attendants, at 3:50 am on June 25, 1975, Sergeant Gresham and Corporal Leary met PC Rayment in the underground parkade beneath Eaton's at Granville and Georgia. The lot attendants directed them to a green 1972 Buick Centurion, which contained the body of a woman seated in the front passenger seat. A parking ticket on the dash indicated that the car, which was registered to Frieda Buxbaum, had entered the parkade at 3:45 pm on June 24. The passenger's door was still locked but the driver's door was not and the keys were still in the ignition, but turned off. Her wrists were tied behind her back with her pantyhose; her dress was pulled up above her knees but no subsequent evidence of sexual assault was found. Her purse and its contents were scattered about her feet, which were also bare. There were no real signs of a struggle. Some blood was found about her nose and mouth and on the two wound marks on the right side of her throat.

Gresham, Leary and Rayment then turned to the Metro Ambulance paramedics who had been summoned by the police dispatcher, as a matter of course. The lot attendant had merely said that there was a woman who was either sick or intoxicated in a car in the lot. Upon their arrival, one of the paramedics entered the car through the driver's door. He checked the woman's pupils and felt for a carotid pulse in the neck; he found neither. He did not move the body but withdrew to await the arrival of the police

Questioning now turned to the two lot attendants. The senior attendant said that he and his partner had started their rounds at approximately 3:15 am, checking the cars which had been left in the lot overnight. At 3:20 or so, they came to the green Buick on level P2. They thought that the woman was either sick or intoxicated, but they rapped on her window without any effect. Neither attempted to enter the car but went directly to a phone and called the police.

Inspector Russ Cumming arrived shortly after with a copy of a missing person report which had been filed at 1:17 am by Elizabeth Markert, who had reported that Mrs. Buxbaum had left during the previous afternoon (June 24) to go shopping and had not returned. Her husband Helmut owned and operated a restaurant on the city's West side.

Detective Cliffe and other members of the Homicide and Robbery Squad inspected the scene at about 4:30 am. The victim had not yet been moved. Close inspection indicated that the wounds on her neck were actually teeth marks; the usual photographs were taken. PC Campbell dusted the outside of the car for fingerprints. The victim was removed by Metro Ambulance to Saint Paul's Hospital Emergency Ward, where at 6:12 am, a staff doctor pronounced the victim dead. Campbell searched the interior of the car for additional prints. That done, Cliffe then removed and tagged for identification a number of items from the car. The only one which was significant was the deceased's white purse, containing a wallet, found upside down between the victim's right leg and the passenger door.

Certain other articles were removed and tagged, even though no one expected that they might be of value: some white granular material was found on the passenger's side backseat. It, too, was saved as thoroughness was uppermost in everyone's mind.

PC Campbell obtained a good clear thumb print from the middle of one of the plastic credit card holders in the wallet. At this point, the car was towed to the police garage for further investigation.

The autopsy began at 9:15 that morning. The pathologist cited the cause of death as asphyxiation due to a crushed larynx. The Coroner's staff took photographs of the bite marks on the neck at half-hour intervals on the instruction of a forensic dental surgeon who had been called for his advice, but this led nowhere and was soon dropped.

At 1:30 pm, the victim was formally identified by her brother-in-law as Frieda Buxbaum.

At 2:50 pm, Cliffe and the city analyst went to the police garage, where the analyst took various samples, including blood from the driver's seat.

The Identification Squad had no luck in cross-checking the thumb print from the wallet with our local records of known criminals, so they wired it to the RCMP 's criminal data clearinghouse in Ottawa; by 10 o'clock that evening, Cliffe knew that he was looking at the left thumb print of Glen Wayne Jansen, alias Robert Allan Street. The search began to quicken, as local justice system records indicated that Jansen was due to appear in court at 9:30 am on June 26 on a charge of auto theft. Homicide and Robbery officers went to the courtroom but found that Jansen had failed to appear and a bench warrant was issued against him for failing to appear and for breach of parole.

His rap sheet listed a butterfly tattoo on the inside of his left wrist, and Det. Glen Clement now learned that he had a cast on his right leg. The white granular powder from the rear seat had been identified as Plaster of Paris; Jansen, as a federal prisoner, was entitled to receive medical treatment at Shaughnessy Hospital. Staff there had indeed put a walking cast on Jansen's right leg to treat a bad sprain. Geoff

Hilton ran comparison tests between the sample from the car and that obtained from Shaughnessy's stock of Plaster of Paris; their characteristics were so similar as to be identical.

A public appeal for information brought in several useful items; most telling was that of an dental assistant who had been followed by a man with a leg cast as far as the elevators as she was entering the stores. She identified Jansen from a mugshot photo. From his co-workers' statements, Clements deduced that after killing Mrs. Buxbaum, Jansen had returned to the project's works trailer and used some of the tools to cut off his cast, fearing that he was too easy to spot while he wore it.

Underworld informants led us to Judy Kingston, Jansen's girlfriend, so permission asked for and received to tap her phone. The tap operator reacted to the audio-visual alarm attached to her line on July 20, 1975. After determining that it originated from Edmonton and requesting Alberta Telephone to conduct a trace at their end, he listened in as the conversation was automatically recorded:

He: ...I can't come back to Vancouver as I could never be a free man again.

She: It's too bad you weren't rich so you could go to Europe and live.

He: Have you had any good dope lately?

She: No, I haven't had any for quite a while.

He: I'm getting $400.00 from somebody and might go down to Calgary next week to see if I can get some...

We notified the Edmonton police, with whom we have a good working relationship and do a brisk exchange trade in used criminals.

At 10:37 pm on July 20, Detective Staff Sergeant Robertson, accompanied by Detectives Boyd, Tetzlaff, Kirkhope and Pearce of the Edmonton Police arrived at Jansen's apartment building at 98th Avenue and 110th Street in Edmonton.

Apartment 4, which was a basement suite, was dark and might have been unoccupied, but as Robertson wanted to know the apartment layout, he and Tetzlaff spoke with the building caretaker while Kirkhope and Pearce watched the windows from the outside and Boyd guarded the hallway to the suite. The caretaker identified Jansen from the wirephoto we'd sent and said that the apartment had been rented to a Miss Heather Haas about one week ago.

With Kirkhope and Pearce watching the windows from the outside, Robertson, Boyd and Tetzlaff entered the suite using the caretaker's key. At the noise of their entry, someone switched on the bedroom light and a naked young woman appeared at the bedroom door, staring uncomprehendingly at the three officers. They quickly moved past her through the doorway, and saw a naked man, who had apparently been sleeping, sitting on the edge of the bed. He did not have a cast on his leg.

Robertson identified themselves as police officers while Boyd and Tetzlaff took him by the arms and stood him up without incident. With the lights on, they were convinced that they had found the right man and arrested him for being unlawfully at large and for suspicion of murder. Robertson immediately advised him of his rights and asked if he understood what he had just been told. "No," he replied, "I don't." Robertson then told him that he did not have to say anything but whatever he did say had to be said voluntarily. The Miranda warning, so common on TV crimes shows, is not used in that form in Canada. The correct Canadian procedure is to advise the suspect of the nature of the complaint on which he is being questioned and to say, "You are not obliged to say anything but anything you say may be given in evidence." Once again, Robertson asked him if he understood, and he now replied, "Yes."

Robertson asked, "What is your name?" Jansen replied, "Douglas Brisson." Repeating the question got the same answer again, so Robertson asked, "Are you Glen Wayne Jansen?" Jansen replied, "No, I'm not." Robertson showed him the wirephoto form Vancouver and said, "Is this you?" Now he gave no reply at all. Everyone was relaxing a bit as arrests like this are always tense; you never know what the accused will do. Jansen was very placid, at least on the outside, but I am sure that he was thinking like mad and was as tight as a drum internally. Tetzlaff, recalling the rap sheet description, turned over Jansen's left wrist and revealed the expected butterfly tattoo: everyone except Jansen relaxed as he was already cuffed and the identification was now complete beyond a doubt. Boyd and Tetzlaff took him downtown, while Robertson, Pearce and Kirkhope stayed behind to question the girl and search the suite. The only thing of significance was a small quantity of marijuana, so she was arrested and taken downtown on that charge.

When Boyd and Tetzlaff got to the CID office with Jansen, they once again asked him who he was and what had happened on the Coast. He now turned sullen and did not even acknowledge that anyone had spoken to him. In the suite, Robertson had asked him if knew that there was a murder warrant out for him and he had said "No."

The interesting aspect of the Edmonton arrest is that throughout the entire process, Jansen never asked once about what was going on, who had been killed in Vancouver, nor did he enquire about any of the circumstances. At no time did he protest his innocence nor did he admit his guilt. He said virtually nothing. His attitude was that of resignation to his fate. He had no symptoms of recent drug use. Marijuana, of course, leaves no external traces but does leave serological evidence in the body for some time, but no blood tests were conducted at this time nor did any of the officers smell any liquor about him.

The particulars of the murder were not discussed with him. Before the trial, his defence counsel would be advised of the exact nature of the evidence and who would be called as witnesses, but no one was going to give him any ideas about how much was known and how much was guessed.

On July 22, Detectives Chapman and Sims interviewed Judy Kingston, who said that she had met Jansen about eight months earlier and had become engaged after about a month. What was of most interest was Jansen's behaviour on June 24 and 25, 1975:

'I came home from work about 5:20. Wayne was waiting and said that he'd been here since 3:30. He looked normal but I can't remember what he was wearing. I asked him what he'd done all day. He said that he'd been to see his doctor (Jansen had sprained his right ankle sometime earlier and it was then still in a cast) and that he'd also enquired about his Workman's Compensation cheques; both offices are on West Broadway. We ate supper and spent the evening with his parents, who came over at about 7:30.

'The next day, he was all dressed up when I came and he said we should go out to eat. We returned about 8:30 and later, close to 10:30, the phone rang. Wayne answered it and spoke to my sister Connie, who was calling to see if we still planned to go to Penticton for the weekend. Wayne said that the Burrard Centre had phoned her and he left in a hurry. Later, my sister told me that she had told Wayne that the RCMP had been to my parents in Penticton looking for him.

'I didn't see or hear from him again until July 12, when he phoned me. I asked him if he had done it, (murdered Frieda Buxbaum) as the newspapers claimed he had. He said, "It was an accident. I saw her cash a cheque for $500.00 at Eaton's and I followed her to the parkade. I tried to get the money from her but she screamed; I tried to quieten her but the next thing I knew, she wasn't moving. I thought she was just unconscious."

'I asked him if he'd done all those sexual things to the other women and he said, "No, I didn't." I asked if he had strangled her with her pantyhose; he said, "No." I asked if he had cut her throat with a knife; he again said, "No, it could have been scratches." I remembered seeing scratches on his neck before he left and asked, "Did you get those scratches from that woman?" "Yeah," he said, "I guess so."

'He said that he'd travelled 7,000 miles since he'd left but didn't tell me where he was calling from.

'He called once on July 13 and twice on July 15. I asked if he had sex with her; "No." he said. When I asked if he'd taken her pantyhose off, he became annoyed; "Boy, your attitude sure has changed since the last time I talked to you!"

'He called me again on July 20 and said that he'd been to Calgary and Edmonton, looking for dope but couldn't find any. He said he'd call again because he wanted to get in touch with his brother.'

Now, at least, there was a witness who could say that Jansen had freely confessed to the murder. Everyone now waited for Jansen's return from Edmonton.

Upon his arrival in Vancouver, Jansen was charged with being unlawfully at large, failing to appear in court, various violations of the terms of his parole and with murder punishable by life imprisonment.

Detectives Campbell and Clement questioned him at length but he steadfastly refused to say anything:

Q: Do you know where Eaton's parkade is in Vancouver?
A: Yes.
Q: Have you ever been there?
A: I have nothing to say.
Q: Do you know this woman? (A photo of Frieda Buxbaum was shown to the accused)
A: I have nothing to say.
Q: Were you ever in this woman's car?
A: I have nothing to say.
Q: Do you have any explanation to say about your fingerprints being found in her wallet in her car?
A: I have nothing to say.

He consistently said nothing and never confessed to any of the crimes for which he was charged, nor did he testify on his own behalf; what could he have said to help his cause? The taped phone confession was very damning.

On March 24, 1976, Jansen received 30 days on the charge of being unlawfully at large; five months consecutive for failing to appear in court and was re-committed on the murder charge. On April 8, 1976, he was convicted of robbery, indecent assault on a female and gross indecency. On April 27, a stay of proceedings was entered on the charges of theft over $200 and the possession of stolen property. Finally, on May 12, 1976, he was convicted in Assize Court of non-capital murder and was sentenced to life imprisonment, and was ordered to serve a minimum of twenty years before being eligible for parole.

Blown Away

On a quiet day late in February of 1968, a long-standing family dispute erupted. In the Eross residence on Laburnum, four people were comfortably asleep; upstairs were Mrs. Eross and a visiting female friend, in the basement were her 17-year old daughter in her usual room and nearer the furnace on a cot slept another visitor, an 18-year old man. Another younger daughter was away visiting friends at the time. At approximately 12:40 am, the daughter was awakened by a scratching at the window, so she turned on a light and found her estranged father crawling through the window he had forced open. "I love you, but I've got to do it." he said, "This is the only way." He lunged at her, still sitting up in surprise in her bed, and stabbed her three times about the head and shoulders. Dropping the knife, he attempted to strangle her with the lamp cord. As she was losing consciousness, she heard him say, "Good! Good! There won't be too much left when they find you."

Her screams awoke everyone in the house. Her mother and her friend rushed down to the basement, where they met Eross in the bedroom doorway, now armed with a Lee-Enfield .303 rifle. He was trying to load it, but in his rage and excitement, he couldn't do it properly and had jammed the gun. The other woman ran back upstairs to call the police.

In the shadow of the furnace, the young man watched horrified as Eross swung the rifle butt and struck his wife twice about the head and shoulders, knocking her to the ground. He stooped down and slashed at her head several times with his knife before going upstairs.

Upstairs, the phone wasn't working, as Eross, an electrician, had cut the phone wires before entering the house, so the friend had to run next door to call the police.

Eross went to the kitchen, where he took a 3-inch paring knife from the cutlery drawer and attempted to cut his own throat; nerves near the jugular vein control major motor functions, so that it is virtually impossible to cut your own throat. Failing that, he left through the basement door shortly before several police units arrived at the house.

At 12:50 am, Bourque and Madsen arrived at the house, on the heels of PCs Dooley and Hardie. They found Mrs. Eross sitting in the centre of the basement floor, bleeding from several head wounds and mumbling incoherently, or possibly speaking her native tongue, Slovak. In the bedroom, Bourque found Dooley attending to the daughter who was lying prone on the floor; she, too, had several upper body wounds. Both women were in a state of shock. Bourque asked the daughter, "Who did this to you?" and she replied, "My Father! My Father!" "What is his name?" "Arpad Eross," she said. From the appearance of the wounds, it was obvious that the attack was only a few minutes old (head wounds tend to bleed profusely, even if they are really quite minor) and Bourque, anxious to pick up any trail as soon as possible, asked her, "What kind of car does he drive?" "A red Volkswagen fastback." she replied.

Bourque sent Johns and Madsen, of the Plain Clothes Special Squad, who had arrived in the meantime, north on the east side of Laburnum while he and Roberts went south on the same side of the street. Bourque and Roberts found a red VW fastback parked, facing north, at the south end of the lane in the next block of Laburnum. It had been driven recently, as the engine hood was still warm to the touch. Bourque then stationed Johns and Madsen to cover the approaches to the car. Checking the licence number confirmed that it was Eross' car.

The house-by-house yard search continued, with officers checking under all shrubbery and inside any unlocked garages. At about 2:00 am, a man was seen walking out of the east lane of the next block of Laburnum towards Eross' car. On seeing Bourque and Roberts walking towards him, he threw up his arms as Johns and Madsen came up behind him and arrested him. He was still bleeding from his throat wound. Bourque told him that he may be charged with a serious offence, that of attempted murder, and gave him the now-standard warning. Eross' response was to say "You might as well let me shoot myself." Bourque asked him if the VW was his and he said, "Yes," and slapped one pocket to indicate that it held the keys. He said that he had money in his car. On searching his pockets, Bourque found a .303 cartridge and a set of VW keys in his left front pants pocket.

The cartridge appeared to be an Army issue round, which were still common enough in those days; it was tagged in the Report Centre for the Property Office. Eross muttered occasionally, saying once that, "If I can't have my daughter, I might as well kill myself." Johns escorted Eross by Metro ambulance to Vancouver General's Emergency Ward for attention to his neck wound, where he was later interviewed by Sgt. T. Brown. Eross said nothing very coherent to Brown, muttering in Slovak or lapsing into periods of silence which grew longer as the interview proceeded.

Meanwhile, Dooley and Hardie had interviewed Mrs. Eross and her daughter. Mrs. Eross could not remember anything that happened after she entered the basement. She said that she had phoned her husband the day before, February 26, and that he had said that he was going to kill her and their daughter.

Mrs. Eross had been struck near the left eye and on the right shoulder by the rifle butt. Both she and her daughter had lost consciousness at the hospital. Mrs. Eross' coma lasted approximately 10 hours, while her daughter's was much shorter in duration. When she regained consciousness in the hospital, Mrs. Eross had complete amnesia for the events of the preceding night.

The daughter had three stab wounds: the one just below the right ear accounted for a great deal of blood loss; there was a small wound behind the right ear and another on the upper portion of the right shoulder blade. The most serious of her injuries was a fracture of the second cervical vertebra, which resulted from the attempted strangulation. There were bruises on her right shoulder and upper arm, probably sustained in resisting her father's attack. She remembered everything up to the onset of strangulation. Her next recollection was that of awakening in the hospital.

The couple had been legally separated since December 29, 1967, although Eross had moved out of the house on Laburnum in August of 1967, and had been living in the 1500 block East 10th Avenue. During their fifteen year marriage, Eross had assaulted his wife several times. After an assault on July 16, 1967, she called for police assistance. Under the terms of the Separation Agreement, he was instructed to pay her $200.00 per month; this, plus other long-standing grievances, may have been the reason for the latest attack.

On March 1, 1968, Bourque called at Eross' East 10th address and spoke to the landlady. She gave him several letters, apparently written by Eross, which she had found in the garbage. These letters, although hard to decipher, indicated that he was planning the actions which he later took.

The evidence was straightforward, and Arpad Eross was convicted on two counts of attempted murder, two counts of causing bodily harm and one count of possession of an offensive weapon and sentenced to ten years in prison. On appeal, his sentence was reduced to 4 years. He was transferred from the B.C Pen to the medium security Le Clerc prison in Montreal to serve his time.

Eross was forgotten until the Vancouver Police received the following letter.

February 20, 1973

Dear Sirs:

On the night of 26/27 February, 1968, Arpad Eross, who was my husband, from whom I had a legal separation, broke into my house, attacked our 17-year old daughter and myself and left us for dead. This was premeditated and not done in the heat of the moment.

On the 12th of March his year, he will be free; not on parole, but free. He is in Quebec serving out his sentence right now, but I doubt he'll stay there after he is out.

Is there anything I can do to ensure any kind of protection? I don't mind admitting we are scared, or at least apprehensive of the future. The Parole Board in Ottawa suggested I contact you. Do hope you are able to advise me.

Sincerely,
Mrs. Eross

As a result of this letter, Nick Lohin and I were assigned to watch the Eross residence.

Our preliminary investigation revealed her suspicions were well-founded. In jail, Eross had always made threats to do away with everybody connected with his case: judges, lawyers, policemen and family. We submitted the following report on March 5, 1973.

'In a letter sent to this department, Mrs. Eross informed us that her ex-husband, Arpad Eross, is being released from Le Clerc on March 9, 1973 and she fears that he will return to Vancouver to murder her and her two children.

'Review of Case 68-9055 confirms that her fears are well-founded. In February of 1968, Arpad Eross broke into the house armed with a rifle and beat Mrs. Eross unconscious and stabbed his 18-year old daughter and then wrapped a cord around her neck, breaking on one of her vertebrae. Both victims miraculously survived this attack. Arpad Eross also attempted to cut his own throat but was unable to inflict a serious injury on himself. He has been confined to correctional institutes ever since and did not apply for parole even when he was eligible, so he will shortly receive an unconditional release. This man is considered very dangerous. Arpad Eross is an electrician by trade and was able to cut the telephone wires prior to entering the last time. B.C. Telephone has been notified and are going to try and hide the wires entering the house.

'Mrs. Eross was separated from her husband prior to the attack in 1968; their divorce is now final. She and both of her daughters still live in the same house.

'We suggest that this woman and her family be supplied with one of our portable police radios and that all police officers in the area be advised of this man's release and that any distress call heard from these premises be treated as an extreme emergency.'

The request for the portable police radio was denied although a silent alarm was installed which could be triggered at Police Headquarters by just touching a button and, remembering Eross' electrical background, the wires were well-hidden.

We felt that Eross was extremely dangerous so we issued this bulletin prior to his release from prison.

'On February 27, 1968, in the 6800 block Laburnum Street, Arpad Eross, broke into his estranged wife's house. He had cut the telephone wires prior to entry. He had a .303 Lee Enfield rifle with him as he entered his 17-year old daughter's bedroom. He produced a knife and stabbed her three times, twice about the right ear and once in the back. He then tied a lamp cord around her neck and choked her, fracturing her neck. She also received a blunt instrument-type injury to her upper right arm and shoulder.

'As a result of her screams, her mother came down to her bedroom and was accosted by her husband, who struck her on the head with the gunstock. A neighbour saw him attempting to load the rifle but he had some difficulty with it. He went upstairs, looking for his other daughter, whom he could not find. He then went into the kitchen and attempted to cut his own throat with a small paring knife. He left the house and was apprehended later in the neighbourhood. He was convicted of two counts of attempted murder, two counts of causing bodily harm and one count of possession of an offensive weapon.

'On March 12, 1973, Arpad Eross will be released from Le Clerc prison in Montreal, where he has served his full sentence. He refused parole as he did not want any restrictions placed on his movement and activities upon his release.

'Mrs. Eross has contacted the Department requesting assistance, as she still lives at the same address with her two daughters, now aged 17 and 22 years. She feels that her husband will return to 'finish the job.' B.C. Telephone has been contacted and their lines to the house have been changed so that they cannot be tampered with in the future. Arrangements are being made to have an electronic sentry installed in the house, the details of which will be forwarded when available. Mrs. Eross and her daughters have been instructed and advised on procedures to follow in the case of an emergency.

'It is requested that any police call to this address be treated as an extreme emergency. The neighbours on both sides of the house have similarly been advised. **SPECIAL ATTENTION is requested at all times of the day and night.** The Report Centre staff are also aware of the situation and will give any call relating to this property priority treatment.

'It is not expected that Eross will return to Vancouver immediately, although this is possible, but the above caution should be continued over a period of 2 to 4 months.

'A photo and description of Eross is attached.

'If this subject is checked by police at any time in the Vancouver area, a full report must be submitted to Detectives Welsh or Lohin.

'Do not arrest this subject without strong probable cause, as he has served his full sentence and is not on parole.'

When Eross was released from prison, the Montreal police put him under surveillance but observed nothing suspicious so they assumed that he was going stay in the Montreal area. We maintained our close surveillance of both the family and their home in Vancouver.

In early October of 1973, we received a report on Eross from the Chilliwack RCMP, and Det. Ray Peterson was assigned to check it out.

He discovered that Eross had arrived in Chilliwack by bus on October 8 and was picked up and taken home by an old friend. Eross told him that he wanted to get some stumping powder to clear some stumps from his parcel of land in Squamish, but he also kept complaining that he had been put away unjustly and was very angry at his family, the judge, the lawyers and the police. Eross knew that his family was still in the same house in Vancouver and he said that he wanted to complete the job he had started.

His friend drove him to Sardis Explosives, but had now grown very suspicious and he asked the sales clerk to say that she couldn't sell him any dynamite without a permit. Eross questioned this but she said it was a fairly new regulation, about a year and a half old. Eross shrugged and left with his friend. He told his friend that he would never go to jail again; if he was caught, he would blow himself up. This only reinforced the friend's concern over the matter and he went to the RCMP. They swore out a warrant for Eross' arrest under a section of the Criminal Code concerning the use of explosives to endanger life or cause serious damage to property but by this time Eross had dropped from sight.

We had traced Eross to an address in the 5800 block Victoria Drive, where he spent two weeks prior to contacting his friend in Chilliwack, but after that, nothing more was heard until November 19, when his friend reported to the RCMP that sometime during the day, Eross had removed the personal possessions that he'd stored with him. He felt that Eross was on his way to Vancouver to kill his family.

Search as we might, we couldn't pick up his trail. The watch on the house, which we'd renewed in October, continued.

At 6:30 pm, on November 23, PC Prion and Policewoman Frazer answered a sudden death call at the intersection of 43rd Avenue and McKinnon Street, in southeast Vancouver. Residents had reported that a tremendous explosion had rocked the area and that a man had apparently been blown up in the intersection.

The body was very badly damaged; but palm prints enabled us to identify the victim as Arpad Eross, whom we suspected had been on his way to blow up his family when the bomb exploded prematurely, killing him instantly. A .25 calibre Colt automatic pistol was found some distance from the remains, and more ammunition was found in one surviving pants pocket. He had been crossing McKinnon to board a waiting bus; we were thankful that he hadn't made it, for the carnage would certainly have been much worse in the enclosed space of a crowded bus.

Evidence gathered at the scene and from eye-witnesses suggests that he was carrying one or two sticks of dynamite in a container similar to a shaving kit, which was triggered by an electric blasting cap. Certainly, an old-fashioned fuse that had to be lit would not have reacted in this manner. Acting on the assumption that Eross had to be staying somewhere in the South Vancouver area, an appeal was made through the media to try and locate his lodging, since he might have left additional explosives there.

The .25 Colt, serial 45859, was checked through local records, the Canadian Police Information Centre in Ottawa and the National Crime Information Centre in the U.S. without any luck. It was retained for a while in the Science Lab for possible comparison tests, but it appeared never to have been reported stolen nor involved in any criminal activities. It may have been obtained by Eross, perhaps even legally, in eastern Canada before his return to B.C.

The search for Eross' residence went on until December 17, when an East Indian landlord decided to check the basement suite he had rented to a man in October, but for which he had not received the December rent. The tenant, who called himself 'Ron,' had said he worked for the Pacific Great Eastern Railway. The landlord looked through the room and its contents, even touching some of the explosives before it suddenly dawned on him that this might be what the radio and TV were talking about. He was indeed fortunate, because he had handled some electric blasting caps which Eross had left connected to batteries! Obviously, Eross was not as conversant with explosives and electricity as he thought he was.

The landlord phoned the police at 6:50 pm, and Nick and I drove out immediately; we were met by PC Anderson and Acting Cpl. Borevitch, who had responded to the original call from the landlord. Borevitch had retrieved various legal documents from the room; included in these were a list of Crown witnesses and the list of Eross' targets, which included those officers involved in the 1968 case.

When we realized the hazards involved, we had the house evacuated and called acting Sgt. Anderson, who called Insp. Baird and Geoff Hilton. After Hilton had taken a quick look, he told us to call in the explosives experts from the Chilliwack army base to dispose of the dynamite, and after tagging and removing the documents, he left. Hilton, who appeared to be very brave with those damned things, had been called away from a Christmas party, and wasn't going to touch any explosives even with only one drink in him. Under the circumstances, nobody wanted to just stand around and wait. Nick and I, however, had no such choice.

I didn't like the look of the dynamite as it was beginning to leak nitroglycerine. Dynamite consists of nitroglycerine and some de-sensitizers in a mixture of Fuller's earth and sawdust, rolled into a stick and wrapped in heavy wax paper; as its shelf life expires, it starts to leak nitroglycerine and should be disposed of because it may become unstable and explode. The leaking nitro fumes can cause severe headaches; (in tiny doses, nitro is used as a heart stimulant) the standard disposal method is to burn it in an open flame. Unconfined dynamite is still dangerous but, contrary to so many B-grade westerns, cannot be detonated by the impact of a bullet when it is in a normal state.

The bombs were to be activated by pressures switches; this could explain Eross' death, if he accidentally shifted his grip on the bomb, he might have detonated it.

The Bomb Disposal Squad eventually arrived. As a matter of course, when we were introducing ourselves to them, I shook hands with the Master Warrant Officer in charge; I was taken aback to discover that part of his right hand was missing. Was that the result of a less than successful disposal? In spite of the nitro fumes, he immediately lit a cigarette, and began inspecting Eross' handiwork. These graphic reminders of the tremendous power sitting poised in that room did nothing to settle my nerves. When he discovered how touchy the bombs were, he used a fishing rod to pick up and transport each one to the robust disposal containers in their truck.

Each bomb consisted of several sticks of dynamite, blasting cap, batteries and assorted nuts, bolts, screws and assorted metal bits packed around them to act as shrapnel.

There were pressure switches but no timers on any of them. A total of 23 sticks made up the six bombs; additional loose sticks brought the total to 80 sticks. The Bomb Disposal Squad said that this amount of explosives could have blown the house completely off its foundations, if detonated. All the bombs were motion-sensitive; they would explode if moved or lifted after being set in place. Obviously, these are very dangerous and difficult to deal with.

After an hour and a quarter, the Bomb Disposal Squad departed with the bombs and loose dynamite for disposal at their training range near Chilliwack.

After they left, Lohin and I removed all of Eross' personal belongings from the room, including several electrical clips, various lengths of wire, mercury switches, pressure switches, other assorted electrical items, a Balaclava-style ski mask and a pair of dark glasses. As we were tagging these items for delivery to the Property Room, I found a paper bag full of blasting caps. I was carefully emptying the bag onto the bed, when a brilliant flash went off in my face! But there was no explosion, so when my eyes adjusted, I looked around and found a newspaper photographer leaning in through the basement window preparing to take another flash picture! Bloody Hell! I could have killed that bastard.

It is sad to say, when looking back on the death of a man, that the survivors were better off for his death, but in this case, it was true; and no Court decision could have ever resolved the issue as satisfactorily and with as much finality as Eross' own fatal error. Thus ended an intriguing case that had far better final results than the courts could ever have managed.

How to Investigate a Rape

Very little has been written on the subject of the rapist and the police.

The first police officer on the scene is very important. He may arrive on the scene by chance or as the result of a radio call, but his immediate actions can set the tone for the rest of the investigation.

The officer must quickly assess the state of the victim, both physical and mental, noting whether the victim is calm, hysterical or in shock. If the victim is injured, the ambulance or inhalator should be summoned, as required. Note the state of the victims clothes. If possible, get the description of the assailant broadcast promptly. Cordon off the site and wait for the arrival of the police dog. Many suspects are arrested hiding in a lane or park very close to the attack site.

Major Crime Scene - Evidence Preservation

The duties of the first officer at the scene of a major crime, such as rape or homicide, are many and varied.

The following is a brief guide which is designed to promote proper evidence preservation and may serve as a basis for the initial investigation of the incident.

1. Safeguard the crime scene by cordoning off the entire area. Anyone, including officers not actually engaged in the investigation will be excluded from the area. Record the names and badge numbers of all officers who, at any time, have come in contact with the protected area.

2. Hold all witnesses separately and limit conversations between them.

3. Hold all suspects separately. If any suspects are present at the scene, they should be removed promptly and taken to Headquarters for interrogation by experienced investigators. Never return a suspect to a crime scene, as witnesses may still be present there, and seeing a prisoner, they may assume that he is 'guilty.' Each investigator must

decide whether, at some later date, taking a suspect to a crime scene will be beneficial.

4. Contact the Chief Despatcher, who will notify the appropriate specialists and squads, such as Identification, Major Crime, the Station NCO and the Field Officer.

5. Make a careful sketch of the scene and note any peculiar or unusual items or pieces of evidence; bloodstains, signs of a struggle, weapons, etc. Weather conditions such as rain or snow can alter or obliterate evidence before a police photographer can arrive on the scene. Though it seems pointless to say so, do not move or touch anything.

6. One officer and one officer only, the Evidence Officer, shall be placed in charge of all the exhibits.

7. Detailed notes should be made on all aspects of the investigation, including such things as the names of all persons present, all relevant times, the condition of the scene, and in homicide cases, the condition, description and location of the victim.

8. A breathalyzer test shall be administered to those involved in the incident, including, if desirable, the victim.

9. In the case of sexual offences, such things as medical examination (which requires parental consent for juvenile victims), seizures of clothing for examination by the City Analyst and the collection of 'Recent Complaint' statements are all essential to the investigation.

10. In the case of a homicide, the first member on the scene will be responsible for completing a 'Homicide Case File,' which will be supplied by the attending representatives of the Major Crime Section.

11. A brief Investigation Report, giving a minimum of information, is desirable in the first instance. A full report will then be submitted, detailing all facets of the incident and subsequent investigation.

Examination of the Scene

1. Doors - locked, bolted, broken, where are the keys?
2. Windows - open, closed, dirty, blinds drawn, broken?
3. Mail Box - any mail, how old, in right order?
4. Deliveries - milk bottles, newspapers, circulars?
5. Outer Clothing - in closet, on body, missing?
6. Lighting - on, off, all in working order?
7. Meters - take readings
8. Appliances - are any left on?
9. Garbage - when is pick up, contents, location?
10. Ashes - furnace, fireplace, stove, ashtrays?
11. Heat - normal, night settings, embers, etc.?
12. Food - prepared, dirty dishes, routine?
13. Odours - liquor, tobacco, perfume, gunpowder and others?
14. Clocks & Watches - going, on time, when stopped?
15. Calendars - any dates marked?
16. Addresses - phone books marked, lists, mail?
17. Sinks - condition, contents, contents of traps?
18. Bathroom - towels, missing, stained, toilet contents?
19. Damage - to anything?
20. Refrigerator & Medicine Cabinets - contents?
21. Struggle - indications, marks?
22. Nude body - where are clothes, are they all present, in what order?
23. Suicide note - instrument used, comparison samples of handwriting?
24. Garden & Yard - signs of fresh digging or paving?
25. Compost, Manure Heaps & Outdoor Privies - has anything been pushed into these to hide it?
26. Tracks - tires, footprints, animals?

Transport the victim to the hospital, or, if the victim wishes, to his or her own doctor, but make sure that sufficient evidence of the correct type is collected, properly identified and turned over to the Police Analyst to support a case in Court. Hospital staff see far more rape victims than general practitioners and soon learn what procedures to follow; a well-meaning general practitioner may overlook something that could be of importance later. Get a verbal report from the doctor immediately after the examination; make sure that it is promptly followed up with a detailed written report.

Take as much of the victims clothing as is desirable for serological examination. Wherever possible, do these things yourself; avoid asking nurses for assistance. It is felt that hospital staff will be co-operative as long as their involvement is minimized to the point where they may only rarely be called as witnesses; if every treatment or examination given in connection with a crime brought them into court, they would soon become unco-operative. Have the victim hand you the clothing. Take careful note of identifying marks on clothing. Deliver clothing as promptly as possible to the City Analyst; If the incident has occurred on the night shift, store clothing in a Science Locker. Attach a copy of the preliminary report, including case numbers, victim's name and an itemized list of the articles of clothing which are to be examined.

If a suspect has been detained, note any injuries, his attitude and general behaviour. Take appropriate items of the suspect's clothing in his presence, list them, and place in Science bags, separating if necessary. Never get victim's and suspects clothing near each other!

The victim's statement should include the victim's address, home phone, place of employment and phone number and details of next of kin. Phone the report in. A copy must go to the victim as well as copies to the Duty Inspector and the Detective Office. If possible, notify the Detective Office immediately.

If you are the first person on the scene, do not put words in the victim's mouth, let them use their own expressions. Later, discreetly question if they have reported rapes before or if she is a prostitute or has suffered from mental illness. This line of questioning was certainly employed in the past; its use today might be considered an invasion of privacy or an infringement of the individual's rights. Ask when she last had intercourse and when she last menstruated. State whether you believe the complaint to be legitimate, and give your reasons for any doubts you may have.

The report must contain a description of everything that the suspect, did no matter how vulgar – this behaviour may provide clues to the identity of the suspect.

In almost all rape cases, the suspect has come into contact with the police on previous occasions; this will invariably come out after the suspect is apprehended.

The goal of rape investigations is to locate the perpetrator as soon as possible to save further victims, some of whom may be young children, from such attacks. The following methods are suggested for rape investigation squads:

1. Modus operandi card files of all persons charged with or suspected of a sexual offence. One-third of all sexual offences could be solved by recognizing the modus operandi of previous offenders.

2. Photos of all persons charged with or suspected of a sexual offence.

3. All serious sexual offenders under observation will be on Canadian Police Information Centre files. This resource has been neglected and is most useful.

4. Make use of the Identification of Suspects files at the RCMP's Criminal Investigation Section, in Vancouver.

5. Maintain liaison with the Police Statistician, whose duty it is to correlate similar offences occurring in Vancouver. Card and file all sexual offenders released on parole, their whereabouts and modus operandi and put their photos in the book. Make it a practice to refer sexual offenders to the Mental Health Clinic. Consult with and seek the approval of the Crown Prosecutor's Office, whose duty it is to determine whether sufficient evidence exists to warrant laying a charge.

6. Investigators must be thoroughly familiar with methods of taking statements from victims, witnesses and suspects. Ensure that suspects have received proper warnings of their rights, so that evidence obtained subsequently will be accepted in Court.

Lectures should be given to the public as well as to new recruits on proper behaviour during an investigation.

This item appeared in *The Sun* on March 18, 1994.

Sex Offenders Escape Longest Jail Sentences

OTTAWA – Many sex offenders received less than the maximum penalty from provincial courts in 1991 - 92, Statistics Canada reported Thursday.

Ninety per cent of offenders convicted of the least serious form of sexual assault got jail sentences of two years or less, said the agency's Canadian Centre for Justice Statistics. The maximum penalty for such a crime was 10 years behind bars.

"Only two out of over 2,000 convictions resulted in a sentence in excess of three years," said the Centre. "It has often been asserted that maximum penalties bear little relation to sentencing at the trial court level."

The figures are drawn from provincial courts in Prince Edward Island, Nova Scotia, Quebec, Ontario, Alberta and the Yukon. The numbers represent 75 per cent of the sentences imposed in provincial courts from January 1991 to October 1992.

The Centre found the majority of convictions for sexual assault in provincial courts result in imprisonment. But the vast majority of the jail sentences were considerably shorter than the law permits.

For example, ninety per cent of those convicted of sexual assaults that involved a weapon or bodily harm received sentences of seven years or less. The stiffest possible penalty was 14 years in jail.

Ninety per cent of offenders convicted of aggravated sexual assault that maimed, disfigured or endangered the life of thevictim received jail terms of 15 years or less. The maximum sentence for such a crime is life imprisonment.

I see nothing wrong with the sentencing provisions the Criminal Code of Canada, but perhaps some judges feel that it is not their ox that is being gored – punishment is not prevention, but it sends a message that society will not tolerate such crimes. You can ask your MLA and MP to press for heavier sentences for sexual offenders, can'tyou?

Pimps and Whores

Being on the Morality Squad for ten years often got me involved in some strange activities.

One task was the apprehension of street prostitutes. This was a foul job and involved following them and their clients, whom they (and we) called 'tricks' or 'johns,' to cheap hotel rooms and listening at the door for sounds of sexual activity. When the trick left, one of us held him while the other would question the prostitute under the Vagrancy Section of the Criminal Code, which has now been changed so that there appears to be no way left to stop street prostitution. The trick was then brought before the prostitute and asked if he paid for sexual intercourse. When he admitted that he had, we could use that as evidence in Court. If he refused to co-operate, he could be summoned as a Crown witness.

Listening at those doors was enough to make you vomit, but it was part of our job.

We met many so-called high-class call-girls who seemed to be immune to prosecution. In the interest of increasing our rate of convictions, I read up on the procedures then being employed in San Francisco and Los Angeles; they were having success with undercover officers posing as tricks, so I suggested this to our Inspector, who immediately said, "Since it's your idea, you get to be the bait!" Maybe I should have seen that coming but now I was stuck.

The first time we tried it, we caught two prostitutes in the lobby of the Hotel Vancouver. The repercussions were very spectacular, as strong threats were made to close the Hotel! Hardly what one expected of the most prestigious hotel in the city, and they had been warned earlier.

The next time, I posed as a businessman from Toronto and found myself in an expensive suite in the West End with Tiffany Lawrence, a prostitute who was a stripper and possessed extremely large breasts. She performed at the Torch Cabaret and could spin her tasselled pasties (this was long before totally nude dancers were permitted) in opposite directions. One of her prostitute friends, Louise Kidd, dropped by almost as soon as we got there. Can you say 'set up?' I knew you could. Not a shrinking violet, Louise suggested, "Why don't we make it a threesome for an orgy?" I was just as happy to arrest both of them, so I asked, "How much?" Tiffany said, "$150." The Department allowed us only $50 in marked bills, so I said, "All I have is $50." The ever-helpful Louise piped up, "You could write a cheque," and she picked up the phone and began dialling Penthouse Cabs to get a driver to drop a blank cheque by the apartment. I was trying to look nonchalant because I knew that there were three detectives listening through the door. So I stepped nearer to the door and said as loudly as I thought I could without attracting suspicion, "Sure, sure; that's great. I'll sign a cheque when the cabby gets here and then we can get started." I was sure I heard the not-so-little scurrying of three pairs of size twelves in the hallway. The cheque arrived shortly and I signed it with my Toronto alias.

Tiffany took off her blouse, bra and skirt and stood there in her panties, looking at me; "You certainly have big breasts," I said. Louise pulled open her blouse and popped one breast out of her bra, "I'm not too bad either." Maybe so, but in that comparison, she finished a distant second. On the pretext of wanting to use the bathroom, I passed the front door and let in Detectives Beatty, Stewart and McGregor. In the angry accusations that the girls flung at them, I whispered to McGregor, "Get the cheque; it's on top of the fridge under some papers." He found it and started to herd us down to the car; Tiffany had started to re-dress automatically but someone had to remind Louise that she still had a big breast hanging out.

At the Station, the women discovered that I was a detective. Louise, whose character seemed to be defined by angry outbursts, was mad as hell but Tiffany started laughing about how they had been taken in, and eventually they both laughed themselves silly, largely because they'd never heard of anything like this before. We didn't tell them how new we were at it ourselves.

These women were all professional shoplifters as well. Every time we knocked over one of their pimps, we'd find lots of stolen goods. Sometimes they managed to steal full racks of coats and suits; at least, they had store racks rather than closets to hang the loot on. As a matter of course, we seized everything we could lay our hands on we ended up giving most of it back as no one could identify it. This lack of positive identification of goods was their biggest ace in the hole, and enabled them to live in the high style they chose. Every suite had crooked cards and dice in it, as all the pimps were professional gamblers. Their favourite trick was to find a well-heeled businessman out looking for fun. Eventually, someone would direct him to the Penthouse Cabaret. From there, a good-looking woman would take him to her suite in the West End for sex, and shortly, some of her friends would show up to play cards. The sucker doesn't have a chance and usually writes cheques to cover his losses, staying longer and longer in the hopes of both winning his money back and having another round with the girl, neither of which ever happens.

After playing all night, they take him to the bank in the morning and cash his cheques, threatening him with exposure and perhaps even phony reports of rape if he seems a little balky. Usually, the sucker is married and doesn't want any publicity, even though he's now figured out that he's been had.

Most of our raids on the pimps turned up the ubiquitous 'little black books,' full of the tricks' names and the dates of their visits, as well as their sexual preferences. The kinkier a trick was, the better they viewed him as a prospect for blackmail. In spite of all the crooked gambling and prostitution that went on, we never had very many people coming to us with complaints about extortion and blackmail. People can be very foolish but they'd sooner rot in Hell than admit just how stupid they've been.

In the wake of these raids, one of the Prosecutors showed up to go through the pimps' books. I thought that he'd been assigned to the task, because at times, he became very aggressive. He was a pain in the ass, so I complained to Staff Sergeant Mel Fish, asking him to get this guy the hell out of our way, since he was actually obstructing our investigations. I never realized until later that he was merely checking to see that his name did not appear in any of those books; what a case of cynical self-preservation. His involvement with prostitutes came to light much later, so his vigilance merely forestalled his come-uppance.

Many prominent men were named in these books. (No, I don't know what became of the books) The whores always entered a guilty plea when charged, so none of these books were ever entered as evidence. Hell, half of the Lower Mainland might have been in the divorce courts if they had been made public.

On another occasion, I went to a West End apartment with a woman. She wanted me to undress and wash my privates prior to intercourse. Again, as I went towards the bathroom, I let my colleagues in the door. The young woman, who came from a very respected family and was a student at Simon Fraser University had shacked up with Bobby Gordon, a known rounder and professional gambler. She entered the usual guilty plea and never returned to that life. She's probably a respectable housewife and mother away from that leech. All that we could do with Gordon was to give him a stern warning about living off the avails of prostitution; a fat lot of attention he paid to that.

The same thing happened again with a beautiful girl whose name was Connie Johnson. She agreed to have sex with me, had taken my shirt off and had led me out onto the balcony to see the sights of Vancouver after dark from her high-rise. Later, I came down with pneumonia and got no sympathy from anyone. Sgt. Jack Bissett said, "Well, Bob, if you were a horse, we'd probably hot trot you – or shoot you."

At that point, I began to think about being out on the balcony, and how easy it would have been for her to shove me over the rail. Most of these women had seen us making the rounds at some time or other, and I wondered about my safety if one should suddenly remember where she'd seen me before. Falling to my death wasn't usually high on the list of on-the-job hazards I had to worry about. In the light of today's hazards, all officers carry disposable rubber gloves for use when handling just about any kind of suspect who seems the least unlikely to go downtown peacefully.

Everyone had to take a turn as the undercover trick. It's funny how circumstances affect a person's behaviour: when it was Staff Sergeant Fish's turn, he became so nervous that the woman, thinking this was his first time with a prostitute, offered him a cigarette to calm his nerves. And Fish, who had quit smoking after a long struggle, gave in and accepted the smoke. In uniform or in plain clothes, but with our own honest identities, none of us were bothered by talking to these women. An alias obviously bothered us more than one ever bothered a criminal. In spite of all this, we gathered the evidence and piled up the convictions. The big distinction between the call-girls and the street whores was that none of the former were drug addicts while almost all of the latter were.

Sgt. Ward Rowan was a very religious person, but not a stereotypical Irish Catholic cop; he was a lay preacher with one of the evangelical churches. One of his talents was the ability to mimic people's voices and he used this during his stint as the decoy. The woman's pimp phoned while she was in the bathroom. Rowan picked up the phone and screamed for help into it; that brought the pimp over in a hurry to protect his "investment." I met him at the apartment door at gunpoint. There wasn't much we could do with him other than scaring the hell out of him. The others gave me the dickens for scaring him with my gun, but later in the week, the same thing happened with a different pimp, but this one came at them swinging a tire iron. Nobody was wearing a gun, so three empty-handed plain clothes officers had to talk the pimp out of attacking them on the spot. Fortunately, somebody knew his name and they avoided a serious incident.

Occasionally, we went undercover in pairs. Ken Stewart and I went to an East End whorehouse, posing as old Navy buddies who hadn't seen one another for a while, and who were out on a tear. The script was in part correct, as we had served together on the HMCS Uganda. The difficulty with these places was mostly in gaining access, as all doors were permanently locked except for whichever door they were using to receive guests. If we broke down a door, by the time we got in, there was nothing suspicious except the presence of several known prostitutes. We'd brought a bottle of whiskey and had a couple of drinks with the Madam, before she brought four women in for us to choose from. My heart pounded because I recognized two of the women and was afraid they'd recognize me. They didn't; while these arrests were usually made without much risk of violence, we still didn't like being discovered and losing the collar. After some banter, Stewart and I made our choices, the women agreed to some specific acts and we paid the Madam in marked bills. We went down into the basement suites. I was to open the side door on the way to use the bathroom, but unknown to me, Sgt. Rowan and Det. Angus Gillies were too far away to see that I had the door open. I waited and waited, making weaker and weaker excuses for not 'getting into action.' Finally, I ran upstairs to open the front door, which I knew was being watched. At the head of the landing, I stepped on the cathouse cat, whose yowls excited the cathouse dog, whose barks brought everybody to attention. I threw open the front door and shouted, "Now! Now! It's open!" There were women running everywhere in various states of dress and undress when Rowan and Gillies came through the front door.

Downstairs, poor Ken had been peeled down to his shorts and was so nervous that he had drank most of the bottle of whiskey. All he could say was, "If you guys hadn't shown up, I would have been in real trouble!" We served our search warrant on the Madam and asked her for our two $20 dollar bills. She hesitated and said, "Search till you find 'em, you bastards!" If we'd lost the money, Inspector Will would have taken it out of our pay and made life miserable for us, but the Madam grudgingly returned the money, there's no telling what else she had hidden that she didn't want us to find by accident.

When we fingerprinted her, we discovered that she had a record of violence and had recently been charged with shooting a man with a shotgun. We could have been killed if things had gone down a little differently. When Ken told his wife Pat about the incident, all she said was, "Ken, I hope you had clean underwear on."

In 1964, Det. Russ Cumming and I were assigned to a case involving the rape and beating of a seventy-five-year old woman in her West End apartment. Two men had entered her suite under false pretences and had helped themselves to some beer. The woman, who was almost blind, was certain that only one of them had touched her, and she described him as a Native Indian. From her description, Cumming immediately recognized the man as a suspect in an earlier rape case. He had been taking a girl to his room for sex, but on the way he had suddenly turned violent and had beaten her viciously before raping her. As is frequently the case with prostitutes, the girl would not press charges.

Forensics took prints from the old woman's apartment. On comparing these prints to those of Hugh Wayne Francis, our earlier suspect, we got a perfect match; he was easily found and arrested. We eventually found the second man, who was a drug addict; his lies on the stand weakened our case against them. The old woman was very confused during the trial and failed to identify Francis but said she could see Detectives Welsh and Cumming in the Courtroom. Magistrate Gordon Scott dismissed the case at the preliminary hearing stage.

Hugh Francis was a known pimp; his whore was Lynn Cherry, a pretty woman who had been a figure skater on Vancouver Island before Francis recruited her to prostitution. One evening, the despatcher sent us to answer a call from her apartment. We were surprised to find her mother there, very upset and crying. Both of her daughters had become prostitutes; the younger one worked for a black pimp. It was quite a sad scene.

"What in God's name did I do to deserve this?" wailed Mother Cherry.

"Don't worry, Mother. I'm the best whore in town." replied Lynn. Hardly a comfort to a distraught mother!

Lynn had phoned in an assault complaint after Francis had beaten the hell out of her. She was afraid for her life, but the attack was several days ago and the bruises were rapidly fading, so an assault charge wouldn't stick. We discussed the case with a prosecutor and we agreed to hide in Lynn's room when Francis came to pick up his money. Lynn had agreed to talk to him explicitly about performing acts of prostitution to support him, and that would give us a strong case against him.

Before we could implement this scheme, justice took a more direct course. Francis had gotten drunk in the Smiling Buddha night club on Hastings just west of Main, and had been thrown out for fighting. He suddenly pulled a gun and began shooting randomly at people up and down Hastings. As you might expect, any gunfire so close to home drew a crowd of officers, though they weren't accustomed to this sort of action. Francis headed towards the Police Station at Main and Cordova, probably intending to take revenge on as many policemen as he could find, with uniformed officers chasing him on foot. He fired at a passing Canadian National Railway Police patrol who were just changing shifts, simply because they looked like regular policemen. During this time, over a dozen shots had been fired uselessly at him, but as Francis turned to face the several officers who were now firing at him, Const. Jack Davies shot him squarely between the eyes. He had committed his last rape and beaten his last whore.

One of the Canadian National patrolmen was a university student working for the summer holidays. He quit on the spot, saying that the money didn't really seem that important any more.

An extensive ring of black pimps operated out of Seattle and Los Angeles. They covered a lot of territory, trying to recruit girls they met in nightclubs up and down the Coast and far inland. The recruiter was usually quite a swinger, a good dancer with lots of money to spend and a recent Cadillac to drive. They would use the older girls to start a young one turning tricks. The newcomer would become the number two or three girl. The pimp's number one girl controlled the others. If any of them got out of line, she and the pimp would beat the hell out of them.

The northern part of the circuit passed through Seattle, Vancouver, Prince George, Edmonton and Calgary. It was so difficult to get conclusive evidence against them that they were virtually immune to the law and made millions. We charged lots of them but usually only after one of the girls had been badly beaten by the pimp.

Vice Squad Sgt. Bill Openshaw, in *The Vancouver Province* of Sunday, October 31, 1993, said that young pimps, especially those from the U.S. are recruiting girls in the suburbs. He cited incidents in Coquitlam. "The more we look, the more pimps we find," said Det. Garry Radons. An American pimp said, "A lot of guys are coming up from the States to Vancouver to recruit girls."

This has been going on for at least thirty years, although it's more likely to have been happening for nearly a century. The law now seems to provide more protection for the criminals than for the law-abiding.

"... and don't tell anybody!"

In those days, at least half of our information was coming in by telephone taps and wire taps. Phone taps are easily understood but a wiretap was a hidden microphone in someone's room. We had our specialists for climbing the poles and making the necessary connections. The Force had a panel truck painted to resemble a B.C. Tel truck but all our work was done at night, when we wouldn't be disturbed by B.C. Tel employees. We had tapped every crook, whore and drug peddler's phone we could find. The active device started a tape recorder whenever the handset was raised from its cradle. There was no approval procedure and no warrants were issued for taps; everybody knew it was happening but nobody on either side was ever going admit it.

Many Eastern hold-up specialists were captured from information obtained in this manner. Whenever one of our stake-outs pulled in a Quebecois hold-up artist, they always complimented us, "You are real gentlemen; in Montreal, we would have been killed. Thank you." It was true in that era; the Montreal Police were the meanest and the quickest to fire at damn near anybody. That attitude has not entirely disappeared; in the early 1980s, the Quebec Provincial Police, acting on a false tip, pulled up to a motel unit thought to hold two bank robbers and machine-gunned it, Rambo-style. The two innocent carpet layers inside were killed. What a stupid mistake not even to have yelled "Police! Come out with your hands up!" It's far better to deal as even-handedly as possible with people until they show that they want to escalate the action. This is easy to say from an armchair but it wasn't the same during those years of duty. Still, reasonable treatment bore fruit in little tips we got from people we'd dealt with over the years. Let's not talk about honour among thieves, but there are crimes that even these people balked at, and their help was always appreciated, no matter how unexpected it was.

Those Quebecois would have fared nearly as badly in Toronto as well. Metro Toronto police had a reputation for being 'rough and tough,' as any old Toronto crooks – any of those that survived – will remember very clearly.

For working the apartments, we had simple earphones and would get a key from the manager, go in and make the connection on the patchboard, usually in a service room. So we knew very well what was going on, we just couldn't use the evidence in court, but it saved endless hours of surveillance. In all my days of listening to whores and pimps and crooks, I never heard anyone mention any Mafia operations in Vancouver or Western Canada. They cannot operate without paying off the police, which was not done in Vancouver. There were, of course, such instances as the 1955 Tupper Commission hearings into graft and corruption in the Force, but the guilt was found to be entirely local and of relatively small extent. If we heard of any suspicious deals involving fellow officers, the Special Squad dogged them until they were caught or they quit the Force.

I remember listening to one whore phoning another from a hospital phone, and saying, "I need pantyhose, nail polish and Kleenex. On your way in to visit me, stop by a drugstore and shoplift them for me, please." Her friend's replies had been barely understandable, and accompanied by various mouth noises, so the shut-in finally asked, "What *are* you doing?" "I'm eating a popsicle; I want to keep in practice for oral sex."

Some phone calls were quite unusual, and many, many of them started out with someone saying, "Don't say anything, this phone is probably tapped." This was like a cue card for us, and almost inevitably, after a few minutes of the usual chit-chat, they would forget their own warnings and start talking in great detail. The whores in particular could never stop talking amongst themselves, and whether they simply listened better or people forgot they were present, they had a lot of interesting things to say. We listened very intently and made the most of the information that we got this way.

The closest I came to being sued arose from a very stupid mistake on a tap in the West End. A known black pimp from Seattle, whose name was Washington, and his whore had rented an apartment. Det. Cumming and I asked the manager for the key to the phone room, explaining what our purpose was. No apartment manager wanted that kind of people in their buildings, so we always got co-operation. Perhaps we didn't stress the secrecy angle enough, perhaps we were a little too explicit in our assessment of Washington and his companion, but when we returned later, to make the connection to their phone, 'Mrs. Washington' met us, in a cold fury. She said that the manager's wife had accused her of being a whore, claiming to have been told that by us. She had phoned a lawyer and there we stood, with well-founded suspicions, but without any local evidence to defend ourselves.

The manager's wife was served with a subpoena and was both very indignant at the thought of 'those kind of people' under her roof and very upset at being named in a slander suit. Cumming and I expected our summonses momentarily, but we were saved by Washington's own criminal nature. He had presented too good a target and was shot in the buttocks during a hold-up in Seattle. Mrs. Washington disappeared southwards and the law suit was dropped.

It was a close call and what we didn't want made public was the nature and extent of our wiretap operations. Hell, everything we did was only to catch crooks. There was no law against wiretaps, and in Canada, evidence was evidence, no matter how you obtained it. The crooks could sue us if we seized stolen property from them after entering their residences without search warrants, but whether we had found drugs or stolen property, the crooks were charged. All this is now changed, and people wonder why it seems that crooks can get away with anything. For a wiretap, you must go before a judge and get authorization. If the evidence you seek isn't obtained within thirty days, the Court sends the suspect a letter, stating that between these dates your phone was tapped in connection with the investigation of specified crimes! That tilts the playing field in the crook's favour.

Abortions

Abortions were another unpleasant duty that brought us into contact with a lot of scum bags.

The Drug Squad alerted us that one of their addicts was to perform an abortion on a certain day; the call had been traced to a West End address. Cumming, Policewoman Ann McKetchen and I staked out the place, waiting for nearly eight hours for anyone to show up. Ann finally said, "This is useless." and left. She'd been gone about ten minutes when the addict, Shirley Tenecke, showed up in her car. Fortunately, Ann's radio was on and she heard us calling for her and returned. We went in with our search warrant, to discover that the abortion had been attempted unsuccessfully the day before and the woman was now aborting.

I phoned Dr. Eric Robertson, the Police pathologist, and asked him to come down and help. He objected vigorously but said he would come and help. By the time he arrived, Ann had hot water ready and the fetus arrived stillborn shortly after. On the heels of this, the boyfriend showed up with a Catholic priest, making the entire troupe look like a circus. All we needed were barking seals.

We searched Shirley's car and found her abortion instruments; she had a hose for shooting soap or God knows what into the vagina and a pair of scissors. Dr. Robertson retained the fetus as evidence; this was probably the first time such evidence was presented in an abortion trial. The victim told us that Shirley said she should have done the same thing for herself, but now her daughter was eight years old. The victim knew that she was breaking the law; she was an employee of the Supreme Court of B.C. At her trial, Shirley Tenecke pleaded guilty and was sentenced to three years in prison.

These amateur 'saviours' were extremely dangerous. Ken Stewart had a case in which a similar method was used and when they entered to make the arrest, they found the housewife had died and the abortionist had fled. They came out to discover that her husband and other children were down the block in a car, waiting for Mommy.

Just after shift change, one evening in 1966, Staff Sergeant Cotter gave Stewart and I a case that had come in from a wiretap; the abortion was to take place at 8:00 in the Abbotsford Hotel. With no time for much planning, we grabbed Policewoman Marilyn Stewart and barely managed to get set up in a room across the hall from the one where the pregnant woman was waiting. A small man came up the hall and entered the room.

As he had arrived empty-handed, we prepared to wait a while before entering. Shortly after, he came out and went downstairs, returning quickly with a bag in his hand. As he went in, another man came out and went into the bathroom at the end of the hall. As I looked out, he stuck his head out of the bathroom door and stared at me. I said to Stewart, "You two go in; I'll nab that guy." As they moved across the hall, I ran down to the bathroom, identified myself, warned the startled man and brought him back to the room.

Ken had unlocked the door with the passkey and threw his shoulder against it. He flew unexpectedly into the middle of the room, since the safety chain we had expected was not hooked up. We were already too late. The young woman lay on the bed with a wire sticking out of her vagina. Marilyn attended to her, Ken cornered the abortionist and I took my man out into the hall. Cumming and a new detective, Ted Rayner, had arrived by this time. My man was trying to talk down his involvement; he said that he'd gotten $50 for renting the room and was going to use it later for sex with his girlfriend - not tonight, Josephine!

"Rayner," I said, "Come over here and be a witness while I seize this $50."

"I don't want to be involved." he said, standing firm.

I couldn't believe it! "We *are* involved; now hold this money and this prisoner or God help you when this is over!"

We nabbed the boyfriend when he showed up and an ambulance was on its way. Marilyn went to the hospital with the young woman, who was already running a high fever, while the rest of us went to the Station.

The abortionist, Lazlo Bandali, was a Hungarian who had served in the German Army in WW II. He entered a guilty plea in front of Mr. Justice Bartman and gave him a long story about how his abortions had helped the German girls who had been raped by the advancing Russian troops. Bartman was of Russian descent; "You did this for filthy lucre in very insanitary conditions," he said, "I sentence you to three years imprisonment." The 'Romeo' who rented the room hadn't been charged as we were going to use him as a Crown witness in the case of a 'not guilty' plea. Fortunately for Bandali, his victim survived the experience.

Marilyn Stewart wanted to quit the Force at this point, as events such as these had upset her deeply. Cumming and I talked her out of resigning and she is now Detective Marilyn Simms, one of Vancouver's finest. When I moved to General Investigations, she was my partner on many morality cases and was a very efficient officer.

Ted Rayner was a real milquetoast. When he was asked to go undercover, he got very upset and claimed he was under a doctor's care for a nervous disorder; since we were more interested in being an efficient unit than in sharing the workload, the wimp was excused – he'd probably have blown cover and wasted all our efforts, anyway. His wife's comment was 'Can you imagine Ted with a whore?' and laughed. I wondered how he had gotten that far in the Force. You didn't need to be a mean, heartless bastard, but you had to have a fair amount of backbone to last at all.

The Special Squad warned us of a rumour that Mrs. Bandali was waiting for us with a loaded shotgun to come and search the house. She also had a previous conviction for performing abortions. She may still be waiting; we didn't need any more evidence and we didn't want the extra risk of being shot at.

When a young woman turned up at St. Paul's Hospital with complications arising from a botched abortion, Ken Stewart and I were assigned to the case.

What was unusual was that the girl had named her abortionist, a Dr. McCallum. We obtained a search warrant and went into his office after hours to tap his phone and, lo and behold, on his desk were two piles of records, one of abortions and one of vasectomies. At the time, the Medical Association frowned on performing vasectomies but they were not mentioned in the Criminal Code of Canada, and so they were legal. His abortion practice stretched from B.C. through Washington and Oregon into California. This was before Roe vs Wade (1973), whose outcome granted American woman legal access to abortions 5 years after abortion was de-criminalized in Canada. We interviewed many of the B.C. women and laid several charges of performing abortions against Dr. McCallum.

Stewart McMorran prosecuted the case and McCallum entered a plea of guilty. McMorran, in his summation, told the Court how good a doctor McCallum was, as he had repaired McMorran's hand after a serious injury and he waggled his fingers to show that it worked fine. His defence counsel argued that he was performing a public service, and the judge, perhaps considering that it was rather rare for complications to arise from an abortion performed by a doctor, while it was commonplace amongst amateur abortionists, gave him a suspended sentence. As we were all well aware, desperate women would go to practically anybody, and it seemed far preferable that someone like McCallum do the job than some addict-whore.

With the removal of abortion from the Criminal Code in 1969, the need for us to perform this unpleasant duty vanished, and we were glad to turn our attention to other crimes.

To Pass the Time

I was a Corporal in the Communications Branch when I was promoted to Detective Sergeant and transferred to the Morality Squad in 1964. Sgt. Joe Cotter was in charge of the Squad. Across the top of the blackboard in his office he had written "Non Illegitimus Carborundum;" I had to ask what it meant. "Don't let the bastards grind you down," he replied.

Joe was one of several storied veterans on the Force. Joe and Det. Ray McIlroy handled a case in which a man reported that his wife had been raped. He had sounded drunk over the phone, and when they arrived at the house, they found that the wife was also very drunk. The story they got was very sketchy, but they handled the case routinely until the examining doctor took them aside to explain his findings. He had removed a wiener from the woman's vagina. This was a new on Joe and Ray, so they went back to the couple and finally obtained the true story. He had come home drunk, only to find that she was drunk too, and supper, which was to have been wieners and beans, was sitting on the kitchen counter, unstarted. They began to argue and to push and shove and wrestle, and eventually, he grabbed the package of wieners and the rest was pretty obvious. Neither had expected that they wouldn't be able to get it out again. Then things got serious; he'd tried a pair of pliers from the basement but being drunk didn't help, and she was getting nervous by then, so they decided to report it as a rape. McIlroy looked at Cotter and said, "Do we have any mustard?"

The Squad was encountering an unusually high number of Black American pimps attempting to recruit local girls as prostitutes and Cotter devised a trick to get the message across that they were very unwelcome in the city. We had brought one of these fellows in for questioning but we all knew that we didn't have enough evidence to charge him, so as we were questioning him in an interview room, the door opened and Cotter came in and sat down across from the man, and never said a word. He didn't have to speak; he just sat there, with his arms folded, staring at the man — dressed in a Ku Klux Klan robe and hood. When we finished the interview, the pimp left and was never reported in the city again. Not approved procedure but it sure worked well.

One afternoon, two PCs radioed in that they had picked up a suspect in connection with several attempts to lure little girls into some of the remaining bush land in the city. They were bringing him even though they knew they had no evidence worthy of laying a charge. It was a standard procedure to try and scare people with such tendencies from getting deeper into crime; we didn't know how effective it was but it had long ago become one of the traditional approaches. Joe must have been feeling extra ornery that day, as he went and enlisted Insp. Percy Easler, head of the Crime Lab, to help him.

The PCs arrived with a huge Hungarian, who claimed to be an ex-Freedom Fighter, wearing a beret and a beard. His distinctive appearance was what had given him away in the first place, and while we were convinced by the children's tales of this man, it wasn't evidence we could use in court. Canada unwittingly received the dregs of Hungarian society amongst the genuine, hard-working refugees, as the Revolution had released their common criminals from the jails along with the genuine patriots. We had enough of them in Vancouver to warrant starting a separate Hungarian Crime Book. Joe had guessed that the man had heard of the terrible torture methods used by the Communist Secret Police in Hungary before, during and after the short-lived 1956 Revolution, and decided to play on his fears.

Cotter had prepared the interrogation room, with towels covering the big tabletop. "Put him face up on the table," Cotter said. As the scene was beginning to appear frightening to the man, it took several of us just to get him laid out and reasonably still. After a short pause, Cotter opened the door, saying, "This is Dr. Easler." He might as well have said Dr. Mengele: Easler stepped in wearing a surgical mask, rubber gloves and silently opening and closing a large pair of stainless steel rib-cutting pliers borrowed from the morgue. The effect was galvanic; the Hungarian began to thrashing about violently, bellowing at the top of his lungs, "No castrate! No castrate! Mercy! Mercy!" It was hard work to hold him down and the noise was terrific. The press room was on the same floor and any kind of unusual noise in the Station always drew reporters like flies. Cotter bellowed, "Shut up and listen!" stepping between Easler and his victim. "We are going to let you go this time but if you ever try to take little girls into the bush again, off they come!" he hissed. With a wave of his hand we all let go and the Hungarian flung himself off the table, bolted out the door and through the growing crowd and ran down four flights of stairs and was never seen in Vancouver again. It is a wonder that we managed to regain our composure to walk out through the curious crowd and that no one downstairs had attempted to arrest the man as an escapee, because he certainly was escaping, in his own mind. The official report stated that "...the suspect was warned and released."

Some may consider that in these two cases we violated people's civil rights; what of the rights and feelings of girls trapped into prostitution and child rape victims? Our sole aim was to protect the populace from those who would harm them. Crime is an exercise of power through fear. We played on the fears of these people to protect the law-abiding and personally less-powerful.

Cotter's policy was that there were no secrets in the squad; if anyone had information, it was made available to all other Police agencies, as we were all on the same team and couldn't be sure that our cases were unconnected with other cases. As such, our office was the centre of a lot of activity. We were visited on occasion by Alf Gunn, who represented the FBI in Vancouver, Johnny Johnson of the U.S. Border Patrol, Harold Halverson of the U.S. Immigration Department and numerous officers from other Canadian police forces, including our Immigration Department. It may sound strange, but at that time, the U.S. agencies would never reveal anything to one of their fellow agencies without an order from someone high up in the Justice Department. The RCMP were just as bad; North Vancouver wouldn't reveal anything to their Burnaby or Surrey branches, but gave it to us instead and we relayed it to them.

Cotter, who had quit drinking some years before, used to take some kind of medicine for his stomach. Whenever Inspector Will dropped, by Cotter would pull out his desk drawer and take a gulp of the stuff, saying. "It's you, Will, upsetting my stomach." Will would reply, saying, "Cut out your act, Joe." Later, when Joe had become an Inspector in Traffic, he came by the office and said, "I have been sentenced to die; the doctor says I have stomach cancer and have only a short time to go." We were stunned. And sadly, when Joe died a short while later, we lost a fine friend and policeman.

At this time, (1968) the brass decided to split up the Morality Squad. Rapes and indecent assaults went to General Investigations, while prostitution, procuring and living off the avails stayed with what was left of the Morality Squad. I went to General Investigations, not realizing what a horrible mistake that would prove to be, and found myself working either a 6 pm to 2 am or midnight to 8 am shift.

The squad was so busy that I worked alone for a long time, and they booked all the rapes and indecent assaults to me. I had to be in court nearly every day, as all my rape cases went to the Supreme Court of B.C. Finally, Bill Davy was promoted to Detective and was assigned to General Investigations. The Inspector, Al Shepherd, said, "He's known to be hard to work with but can you use him as your partner?" Bill had spent his 16th birthday overseas with the Canadian Army during World War II; when he returned after 5 years in the Army, he still wasn't old enough to drink, to vote or even to join the Police Force! When I joined the Force in 1950 and worked the same shift with him, he had been a policeman for three years. We worked well together and became good friends. As well as rapes and indecent assaults, we also handled knifings, serious assaults and night hold-ups. I think that we became stressed out with this strenuous routine.

Charlie Ball made Sergeant and joined us. Although he had very little investigative experience, he organized the best parties amongst ourselves and the Homicide and Robbery Squads. We partied at the Sergeant's Mess at the Seaforth Armoury. We never drank on the job but we were all drinking heavily at the time. The stress had made us rebellious. I threatened to punch Staff Sergeant Roy Tabbutt, as he kept bugging me that I was friend of Inspector Norm

Will. I told him to lay off, as I had great respect for Will and would never say anything against him. He got the message and we are still friends today.

Insp. Shepherd wanted to see Bill Davy when we were working the 6 pm to 2 am shift. He came into the Detectives' mess and bellowed, "Davy, get into my office right away!" Davy stood 6'4" and weighed 250 pounds. He picked up Shepherd by his shirt front, dragged him into the next room and threw him into a chair. I closed the door. Staff Sergeant John Page said, "We'll have to go in there; Davy is going to beat the hell out of him." I said, "We will mind our own damn business; if he punches him, then he punches him." Nothing went any further; I don't think Shepherd ever did say what he wanted to see Davy about. In general, we got great co-operation from the supervisors; we worked hard and apprehended many rapists and child molesters.

Page decided to enlarge the Morality Squad and to use me as the nucleus. Staff Sergeant Morphett, who was going to the Cheque Squad, thought very highly of Davy and I, and wanted to take both of us, but in the end, only Davy went with him. My new partner was Detective Glen McDonald, whose father had also been a Detective on the Force.

McDonald was very sharp and a great typist and report writer. Report writing was my weakness. I was the only person chosen who had any previous morality squad experience. Joe Stanton and I started in the Force on the same day: May 1, 1950. In October, 1993, I attended his and Doreen's his fiftieth wedding anniversary.

We kept voluminous files and carded every reported offence in the Lower Mainland. We also had photo books of all the parolees. Upon their release from the Pen, the parolees reported to Insp. Molyneaux, at which point he would call me into his office and we would card the man and add his photo to the book. Seeing them that way, I was soon able to identify most of them on sight, and it was relatively easy to keep them under surveillance.

Hard to Get

1970 was the start of an era of serial rapists.

The Simon Fraser Rapist used to pick up female hitchhikers, take them up Burnaby Mountain to the University where he raped and beat them. The case had been assigned to Stanton and Johnson but they were out when his latest victim came in with her jaws wired shut. She was in pain but was angry and determined. "I'll do anything to catch this bastard!" she said, "I haven't eaten anything but milk shakes for ten days." The only common thread we'd noticed in his five attacks was that he frequently picked up his victims around Broadway and Main at about 5:00 pm. I suggested that she might recognize him if she hung around that area. She took her male cousin along for security and after a few days, she did spot the rapist as he drove by and got his licence number! The passers-by must have been puzzled, her cousin said, because she became quite hysterical when she saw him, and began to jump up and down and shout through her wired-up jaws. That was all it took; Burnaby RCMP had staked out parts of Simon Fraser for days on end, tying up numerous officers without achieving anything, but one angry, determined victim in the right place was far more effective. Stanton and Johnson made the arrest, and with her eye-witness testimony, he was sentenced to twenty years in the Pen.

UBC and the Point Grey area were also plagued by a rapist who worked on foot, so we suspected that he must live in the area. UBC and the University Endowment Lands are not part of the City of Vancouver, so they are policed by the RCMP. Since all the roads from the campus lead to Vancouver, we often co-operated with them in various operations. Striking about twice as often in Point Grey as on the campus, where he preferred to haunt the trails running through the Endowment Lands, he had victimized ten young women. All of his victims remembered his great strength, which made it easy for him to subdue them and tape their hands, eyes and mouth before proceeding. We resorted to using Policewomen Sharon Smith and Marilyn Simms as bait; they were very pretty but as they carried their guns, they would not have been easy prey. Marilyn remembers that when we asked for her assistance on this case, she realized that this was indeed police work and it was dangerous. Between ourselves and the UBC RCMP, there were numerous officers scattered about the campus. One of their Constables saw a man grab a girl but when he ran towards them, the man easily outran the Constable. But he'd left his bag behind, and it told us that he was attached to the Physical Education Department of Lord Byng High School, which is practically on the northeastern edge of the Endowment Lands, at Sixteenth and Camosun. And he was smart; he immediately reported that he'd just discovered that his bag had been stolen, destroying, at last temporarily, the connection to himself. The RCMP arrested him anyway, and I held a line-up but none of the victims could identify him, not even the one who'd been saved by the RCMP Constable. We couldn't charge him but the RCMP did lay charges, although they were later stayed. We kept a detail on him for some time but as no more offences were committed, we were eventually required to lift the surveillance. Police work, like anything else today, contains an element of cost-effectiveness; if an investigation is going nowhere or the criminal seems to have ceased operations, albeit temporarily, we are reluctantly forced to turn our attention to cases that are definitely still active. However, as he had raped ten women, it hurts me that he is free today – and it is probably correct to say that he has never received any treatment for his aberrant behaviour – so he may strike again.

Rapist are perhaps more creatures of habit than anything other kind of criminal: other criminals are after profit but these men are after the exercise of personal power. Their fixity of purpose often leads us to them but I suspect that they may be largely powerless to change the details of their brutal procedures. One rapist used to pick up hitchhikers in his van. Once they climbed in, they were literally trapped; there were no interior door handles except on the driver's side, not even a handle to roll the windows down. All his victims described the van as a prison and gave explicit evidence of his viciousness.

I salute the courage and presence of mind of anyone who could behave as one of his victims did: she wrote down his licence number as he drove away. We then knew who we were looking for but couldn't locate him. While we were searching, a New Westminster City Detective phoned and said that he was bringing in our suspect, Matheson. Matheson had heard from someone that we had a warrant out for him, and had gone to the Detective, who was a family friend, for advice.

I called the Coquitlam RCMP to advise them of our line-up and to request that they bring in the one victim they had who'd been raped in this type of van. The investigating officer said, "I'll phone her and see if she can get there, but I want you to lay the charge, as I'm very busy." Christ! After an ever so slight pause, I changed the tone of my voice and asked to speak to the officer in charge of the Detachment. At the line-up, I was satisfied to see both the victim and the oh-so-busy investigating officer. From his attitude, you'd have thought he was handling a minor traffic complaint, but she made a positive identification of Matheson.

The New Westminster Detective had told Matheson, "You'll get five years for this." which was prophetic, as that was exactly what he got.

We often encountered officers in other Forces who had strange attitudes towards rape as a crime. We caught one rapist who had used a revolver to subdue his victims, so I checked the files and phoned the Burnaby RCMP to advise them of the line-up. "We've got a suspect going into a line-up that could be your man from the rape at Burnaby South High School." I said. The desk sergeant replied, "We've wiped that one out; we don't believe her story." "Hell," I said, "We've got five similar cases and a suspect with a gun. The line-up is at 11:00 am; bring her down." I hung up without waiting for his reply. The Mountie showed up with the 16-year old Burnaby victim, who went into hysterics when she saw the suspect in the line-up but she calmed down enough to write his number down. "Now," I said to the Mountie, "Do you believe her story?"

Two of our PCs radioed in that they had arrested a man who had been struggling with a woman on the Burrard Bridge. "If you hadn't come along," she told the officers, "I would have been raped and murdered; he said he'd throw me off the bridge when he was done." It was unsettling to discover that this man, Campbell, lived not far from my house in Burnaby; I personally dropped off a copy of the Occurring Events report at the Burnaby RCMP office.

Shortly after, a young woman was murdered near the Pancake House on Kingsway. As a routine procedure, the Burnaby RCMP pulled the files of all known violent offenders who lived in the vicinity. When they reached the report that I'd given them on Campbell, some of the details seemed to fit their crime as well. He was still at large because he had not been charged in the assault on the Bridge. When Staff Sergeant Paul Starek searched his house, he found the murdered girl's ID. Even though his claim that he found her ID was so transparent and we knew that he was as guilty as hell, his lawyer, Ken Young, got him off. The RCMP were as convinced as I was of his guilt and on the day he was released, Starek put a tail on him. One of the female jurors had approached Starek after the verdict had been read and had requested police protection as she, too, feared Campbell. Within hours, they arrested him again in the parking lot of the Dell Hotel in Surrey, where he had attempted to rape a young woman, again telling her that he was going to kill her when he was done. Later, the RCMP phoned and thanked me for supplying the report but were very disappointed when he was acquitted on the murder charge. The best the judicial system could do was to convict him of assault, for which he got much less time than he deserved.

As I've mentioned, the Vancouver Force acted as a clearinghouse for the Lower Mainland so the Burnaby RCMP might have found it eventually, but with a copy of it in their own files, the process ran so much faster. Nowadays, computerized record-keeping and searches make such cross-checking much easier, but there is still a tremendous volume of reports written each year. You can imagine how slow and haphazard the process seemed in the old days before we computerized.

When Glen McDonald was promoted to Sergeant, I got another great policeman as a partner, Nick Lohin. Good partnerships, no matter what the nature of the business, are very important: in police work, they ensure your well-being and sometimes your survival. Another very effective partnership was that of Joe Stanton and George Johnson. One of their cases involved a vicious rape near Robson Street. A teenager had forced his way into a West End apartment at knife point and had raped the young woman he found there. In her struggles to resist, she grabbed the blade of the knife and it cut deeply into her fingers, severing many of the tendons. Stanton and Johnson thought that the rapist might live in the neighbourhood, so they suggested to the victim and her twin sister that they would cruise through the area in the hope of spotting the man. They set off in an unmarked police car. Robson Street was full of pedestrians, many of them decent folks out shopping but there were a lot of male prostitutes and other vermin about, if you knew how to read the signs. After several passes through the neighbourhood, the two women, who had been talking quietly in Swedish, suddenly started screaming and pointing. Stanton and Johnson made the arrest and the man was convicted and sentenced – another good bit of police work.

You hear stories of vigilante groups, citizen's arrests and the Guardian Angels, and though many of these tales are fanciful, Nick and I had the opportunity to see one that really worked. During 1972 and 1973, there had been a number of sexual attacks on young boys in Burnaby and Coquitlam. The attacker always wore a hood over his head and subjected boys about 13 or 14 years old to oral and anal intercourse. Normally, no Police Force wants amateur assistance, but if it is well-thought out and no one gets delusions of grandeur, it can be very useful. A simple patrol, like the old-fashioned and perhaps about-to-return beat cop, can deter and prevent a lot of crime. It is certainly effective against crimes for profit but less effective against sociopathically-driven crimes such as rape. The series of attacks prompted the formation of a citizen's group to patrol various neighbourhood haunts, and it was these people who actually captured the rapist as he was about to strike again. On October 26, 1973, Lohin and I arrested Peter Alan Holman, and charged him with gross indecency and indecent assault on a young boy.

Holman lived in the shadow of Vancouver's City Hall but none of his crimes had been committed in Vancouver, so Nick and I were curious about why he had avoided the City. Holman's answer was deceptively simple: "You Vancouver cops are too smart and well-organized." He had a similar record in Ontario and elected trial by Judge. Holman was committed for trial on January 2, 1974, and was duly convicted and sentenced to a long term in the Pen.

The decade ended with the start of a new and lengthy series of rapes. Women and children were assaulted and raped by a man wearing a paper bag over his head, which earned him the nickname of the Paper Bag Rapist. I retired in 1980, and now split my time between B.C. and Peru, but at one point, based on newspaper stories and phone conversations with friends, I wrote a letter to the Vancouver Police, suggesting that they look at Holman again. You can tell when you are really out to pasture: people who used to be your superiors, colleagues and subordinates ignore your suggestions. To my mind, this seemed like his kind of crime. I never received an answer to my letter but it took them nearly eight years to make an arrest and obtain a conviction of another man in this case.

As useful as records, computers and ever-improving scientific teciques are, nothing seems to surpass the analytic powers of the human mind. An experienced investigator, searching his memory without the aid of a written 'program,' can summon up seemingly unrelated details to bridge the inevitable gaps and often numerous gaps that mark each investigation.

A Stake-out and A Set-up

One night, while we were working the 6 pm to 2 am shift, I got a call from a Richmond RCMP Constable, who said that he was about to go on stake-out in our area, in the 800 block SW Marine Drive.

A few days after the burglary of a Richmond house, someone had phoned asking the owner to meet them at a gas station-convenience store on Marine Drive in order to recover some of his stolen property. The Constable was calling to let us know that he would be operating in our territory. "Are you working alone?" "Yes," he said, "But that's no problem." "Better to be safe," I said, "Wait for us and we'll give you a hand." We met him and he gave us the licence number and description of the homeowner's car. I agreed to take the store; Nick and the Constable were to remain out of sight.

On schedule, the homeowner arrived and parked in front of the store, followed in a few minutes time by three men in a Thunderbird. The driver got out, and as he walked towards the homeowner's car, a family pulled in for gas. I stepped up to the driver's window and said, "I'm Detective Welsh, Vancouver City Police. We're busy here; go some place else for gas—Now!" As he drove off, I turned and drew my gun. "Stop where you are!" I said to the driver, who was part of the way into the homeowner's car. He froze and I turned back to the Thunderbird, yelling, "Get out with your hands up!" As the two men got out, I saw that they were huge, even larger and meaner looking than the driver. In order to cover all three of them, I had to swing my gun back and forth like some crazy caricature of Annie Oakley. Where the hell were Nick and the Constable? I was worried that these guys would think I was as nervous as I really was becoming. Nick and the Constable finally arrived, explaining that they'd positioned themselves to see where they thought the action would take place, but with a very poor view of where it actually happened. Luckily, all three men chose not to resist in any way.

After we'd frisked and cuffed them, we opened the Thunderbird's trunk to reveal a loaded, sawed-off twelve-gauge shotgun. The Constable turned and ran for his car; "Where the hell are you going?" I yelled. "To get my gun," he said, "It's in the back seat of my car." Christ, I thought, don't they teach these guys anything? "Too late for that." I said, "Here, hold this nice shotgun on them."

The homeowner piped up at this point, "That guy hid a knife under the rear tire while you weren't looking!" Sure enough, and we added that to the list of goodies.

We drove the suspects to the Richmond Detachment for booking. The driver, Stephen Long, was the only one carrying any papers but identifying the rest was merely a matter of time. The Constable had just recently been transferred to the Richmond Detachment but he had some 14 years of previous experience; still, it made me wonder about some officers. My report recommended the homeowner for a citation, as he'd done much more than we expected of an unarmed, ordinary citizen.

Shortly afterwards, while Long was holed up in his house in Delta, Staff Sergeant Ron McKay called there with a warrant. Long opened the door and shot him dead with the same sawed-off shotgun that we'd found in the trunk of the Thunderbird. The Richmond RCMP had returned it to him; God help me, I can't figure out why!

Most shotguns, which are meant for shooting ducks or pheasants while in flight, are sold with barrel lengths of 28 or 30 inches. The legal minimum is twenty inches; tactically, such a weapon is used only for riot-control. At close range, they are deadly and frightening. Criminals cut theirs down to make them easier to conceal and quicker to manoeuvre. Even if the barrel was still just over the legal minimum, it should have been seized because it had been altered with intent and had been found in connection with the investigation of a crime. I can't explain the reasoning behind this one, and it cost a decent man his life.

Long was arrested before he could escape and was sentenced to life imprisonment.

The Crime of the Future is Here Today

The crime of the future seems to be serial rape and murder. While such crimes are not new – just what do you think the Pied Piper did with the children of Hamelin? – Jack the Ripper's crimes certainly aren't mythical – but the question remains as to how, or even whether, society can protect itself from those who will follow in their bloody footsteps.

One of the important unresolved issues in analyzing such crimes – to 'understand' them seems beyond the bounds of normalcy – is whether these persons were born deviant or whether they were induced to become deviant by their environment, including the people they encountered on the path to rape and murder. Certainly, some children are born with abnormal brain structures; Down's Syndrome and hydrocephalus have been well-studied, but while they may be associated with some degree of amoral behaviour, they are not the hallmarks of such extreme behaviour. We may assume then, that other, subtler forms of genetic abnormalities exist and may contribute to an individual's predisposition to crime. Considering the vast changes and improvements in our understanding of mental illnesses in the past one hundred years, we may learn as much again in the next century. Society will have to work at it and wait.

We are not talking either of crimes of profit, whether they feed the stomach or an addiction, or of crimes of passion, however accidental – we are talking of coldly premeditated kidnapping, torture, rape and murder. These are crimes of power whose aim is to achieve feelings of domination, superiority and sexual ecstasy at the expense of the dignity, sanity and life of the victims.

The victims are frequently selected for two reasons; they are physically vulnerable, and they bear the unmistakeable aura of youthful innocence. Mythologically, they are sacrificial virgins. Totally absent is the pride of vanquishing an equal or superior opponent in single combat, totally missing is the harmony of a willing, mature and experienced sexual partner – the only thing that matters is the exercise of god-like personal power.

Realistically, we don't even know whether such crimes are growing more common. It is only modern communications and a more general openness in all societies that permits these crimes to be spoken off so openly. And their relative rarity cannot provide any reliable statistics to describe changes in their frequency of occurrence.

Over the years, most major metropolitan cities have been stalked by serial killers; Vancouver, Seattle, Los Angeles, Chicago, Atlanta, New York, St. Catharines (the as-yet to be resolved Paul Teale - Karla Homolka case), Yorkshire, England and a recent case has even come to light in Russia. Language, distance, time and politics affect our awareness of some examples – but are not barriers to such criminal behaviour. Other such people have no doubt lived out their twisted lives without detection. Only God knows how many criminals of all kinds have eluded punishment in this world, only to be shown the 'Down' elevator in the next.

Vancouver Police alone received approximately 300 missing person reports each month in this era – most were cleared up in prompt order, without any sinister or criminal overtones – but there were approximately 5,000 known sexual deviants in the Lower Mainland at that time.

To discuss Clifford Olson is to enter a twilight zone in which everything seems to keep shifting its position and changing it size. What is certain is brutal, what is unknown is frightening and yet intriguing – how does such a mind function? Olson will be discussed in some detail, only because he haunted this part of British Columbia.

...God's forgiven me...

It was the worst of times. The preceding few years had seen society shuddering as the Yorkshire Ripper, the Green River Murderer, the Hillside Strangler, the Freeway Killer, Ted Bundy, John Wayne Gacy and Wayne Williams raped, mutilated and murdered their way into mainstream consciousness. Social unrest bred on interest rates that soared close to 20% in Canada; bankruptcies and mortgage foreclosures, those almost-forgotten spectres of the Great Depression, were widespread, while the job market shrank alarmingly towards the coming economic disaster, which would be euphemized by calling it a 'recession.' A lot of common courtesies and family bonds frayed and finally broke under the strain.

On January 7, 1980, Clifford Olson, 41, was released under mandatory supervision from the Saskatchewan Pen in Prince Albert. He stood five foot six, weighed 160 pounds and had brown hair and dark, animally-penetrating eyes.

In February, he was charged with sexually abusing a 14-year old boy in Vancouver; the charges were later stayed.

Under mandatory supervision, which began in 1970, an inmate was automatically released from custody after serving two-thirds of his sentence; he was not free, but was allowed to finish his sentence on the street and had to report regularly to the Correction Services and the police. Release was automatic unless someone had recognized that the prisoner might cause trouble. It was not parole, because no application was made to a Board, but similar terms and conditions had to be observed. A problem with this approach was that those who were returned to prison for some violation of their release conditions did not incur a further sentence unless they had committed a new crime. The time spent at large was deducted from their sentence. The practice continues today; it is said to save lots of money.

This was Olson's fifth release under mandatory supervision; none had been completed successfully. He had also been paroled unsuccessfully twice.

Olson returned to what he knew best – petty thieving – to support himself. In the twenty-four years since his first arrest and conviction at seventeen, he had only spent approximately 48 months lawfully outside of some prison; a six-time escaper, he had been unlawfully at large for only a few additional days during those years. Police considered him nothing more than a journeyman burglar-thief, and 'journeyman' he was, constantly travelling on the lookout for opportunities – for sex and for crime.

But he still had outstanding debts to pay, and they caught up with him in an unusual way. Moved by nostalgia, on May 8, he joined a public tour of the soon-to-be-closed Pen; he wanted a last look at his old cell. He was recognized and arrested by a guard as a parole violator, entering the books as the last man ever arrested there. He spent his outstanding time in Matsqui prison until July 8, when he was again released under mandatory supervision.

He resumed his relationship with Joan Berryman, a 41-year old divorcée, whom he had met in February. In any case, he avoided further scrapes until his sentence expired on September 7, 1980, and he was then free of supervision. In the meantime, Joan had told him that she was pregnant.

On November 17, Christine Weller, 12, disappeared from Surrey. After disposing of her body near the north arm of the Fraser River in Richmond, Olson's car got stuck and he had to call for a tow truck to pull him out.

Surrey RCMP spent three weeks searching and interviewed over 100 people, but they were stymied. Neither RCMP nor the Wellers made a public statement or appeal at this time; the baffling disappearance was just one family's personal tragedy. The Wellers had been living in a motel and papers suggested that Christine was known to child case workers, so it was easy to assume she was a runaway.

On Christmas Day, a Richmond man, out walking his dog, discovered Christine's nude body poorly hidden in the underbrush near the north end of Nelson Road.

The first tiny newspaper item about the discovery appeared on December 27; larger and larger items followed on December 30 and 31.

On New Year's Day, 1981, in Squamish, Olson raped a 16-year old Surrey girl whom he had picked up as a hitch-hiker; he was charged one week later with rape, buggery, indecent assault and possession of a gun. Olson was sent back to Oakalla to await the trial. Olson's standard pick-up routine was to give the potential victim one of his business cards; it allayed fear because it made him look respectable. However spurious its 'enterprise' may have been, it had his correct address. In this respect, his approach never varied.

I entered my last year of service on the Force. Somewhere ahead, was a point past which my skills and abilities would not be considered in any of the Force's operational decisions. With mixed feelings, I sometimes stopped and looked for it. It crouched out of sight, more obvious by its absence than it would have been if it were in plain sight. It was the worst of times.

On January 3, the RCMP confirmed that the body found in Richmond was that of Christine Weller.

On April8, the sex charges were stayed, in large part because the Crown felt the complainant "...was not believable, a liar and a tramp." Bail was made on the two weapons charges and Olson was free again – for the last time.

On April 10, Joan Olson gave birth to a son, Clifford Stephen. The couple moved into a Coquitlam apartment building on Foster Avenue owned by the company Clifford Olson Sr. worked for as a handyman. Amongst their holdings were four particular buildings; the one on Foster, one each on Smith and Cottonwood Avenues in Coquitlam and a fourth at the intersection of 136th Street and 10th Avenue in Surrey.

The neighbours were surprised to hear Olson claim to be the owner of the building. He was quickly typed by many of the children as a 'creepy bogey man;' he told them to call him 'Uncle,' and offered them candy but got angry when they rejected his proffered 'friendship.' Although it was noted that he was a nice talker, he was also described as pretentious, quick-tempered and hard-drinking. He didn't seem to have a job; sometimes he'd appear wearing a T-shirt and jeans, while at other times, he'd be in a suit, smoking a big cigar. He told one neighbour that he had "...found God." Olson boasted of how much money he had and how he had once owned two construction companies.

On April 16, Colleen Daignault of Surrey, 16, disappeared on her way home from a friend's house in North Delta. Surrey RCMP treated the case as simply that of a teenage runaway, in spite of her aunt's continued insistence that Colleen was not a runaway.

Five days later, Daryn Johnsrude, 16, a visitor from Saskatoon who had been staying with his mother and stepfather in Coquitlam, just a half-block from the Smith Avenue apartment building, disappeared from the Burquitlam Plaza, where he had gone to buy some groceries shortly before noon. By policy, the RCMP were prevented from accepting a missing person report until 48 hours had elapsed from the last contact with the missing person.

After dumping Johnsrude's body, Olson's car got stuck on a bad road near the tiny community of Deroche and a farmer helped pull it free with his tractor. Again, while Coquitlam RCMP began their investigation, there was no public statement. This pattern of an almost routine acceptance of children's disappearances would continue for nearly another two months.

April 27 saw Olson in trouble again; he'd been arrested and charged with shoplifting from a Surrey hardware store. He was released pending a hearing.

On May 2, Verna Bjerky of Yale, 17, disappeared while hitchhiking from Hope to Kamloops. Definitely not a runaway, Verna had not picked up her last pay cheque nor touched her bank account but had simply borrowed four dollars to visit her boyfriend in Kamloops, with her parents knowledge and permission. She was never seen again.

On May 8, the remains of Daryn Johnsrude were found. On the 11th, the RCMP told his mother and stepfather, not in person, but casually over the phone, that he was dead.

On May 15, Clifford Olson Jr. married Joan Berryman, née Hale, in a fundamentalist church in Surrey.

On May 19, Sandra Wolfsteiner, 16, hitched a ride in front of her boyfriend's house in a grey, two-door car and disappeared from Surrey. No public statement was issued.

On May 26, an RCMP cruiser stopped Olson and a 15-year old Coquitlam girl in a car near Agassiz. He was charged with drunken driving and contributing to the delinquency of a minor and released once again.

On June 21, the day after someone had added Olson to the list of possible suspects, Ada Court, 13, disappeared as she was walking home from baby-sitting at the Cottonwood Avenue apartments. No public statement was issued.

On June 22, Olson phoned the Delta Police and was connected to Dennis Tarr. Tarr, the only detective who was working that day, had never met or heard of Olson before. Olson wanted to talk to him about the possibility of becoming a police informant.

Around this time, Olson had approached a woman who lived in his apartment building and asked if he could post a notice for window-washing jobs in the arcade she co-managed in the Lougheed Mall. She later phoned the police when two girls told her that Olson had met them at a construction site and made a lewd proposal. No action seems to have been taken on the complaint.

On Thursday, July 2, Simon Partington, 9, failed to meet a friend near his house and did not come home for dinner. Surrey RCMP began to investigate, assuming it was a routine disappearance, perhaps arising out of some misunderstandings. When his bike was found behind a shopping centre, their efforts escalated. Provincial Emergency Program volunteers searched the surrounding bush, while the RCMP conducted a careful door-to-door canvas of the neighbourhood.

The intensive ground and air search by helicopter had produced nothing and they had appealed for public aid.

A fish and chip shop proprietor told RCMP that Simon had left her shop with a man who had bought Simon some fish and chips. She knew Simon and thought the man was his father until she saw Stephen Partington later on TV. The man was in his early thirties, athletic-looking, well-tanned, blonde and stood five foot nine. "...just a gorgeous man," she said. Who was this man, who was too handsome and too tall to have been Olson, and what role did he play in Simon's disappearance? The question of accomplices, like that of near-victims who were neither molested nor murdered, was to be debated inconclusively for months.

On July 7, Olson enticed a 16-year old Burnaby girl into his car and assaulted her.

By the next day, $5,000 in reward money had been raised in the Simon Partington case.

On Thursday, July 9, Judy Kozma of New Westminster, 14, disappeared; she was last seen at a bus stop on her way to a job interview. Her sister and friends said that Judy had recently been approached by a man in a Richmond mall who had offered her jobs as a window washer and baby-sitter. New Westminster police were convinced that she was a runaway.

On July 10, Surrey RCMP wound down the search for Simon without finding any further trace of him. Olson and his family started south on a vacation trip to California.

On July 15, at a meeting of the principal investigators, three suspects were considered. Cpl. Les Forsythe of Burnaby named Olson as the prime suspect; surveillance was discussed at that time, but no agreement was made to implement it. Five children had been killed so far but only one body had been found. Incredibly, the New Westminster representative at the meeting was either unaware of Judy Kozma's disappearance, or, as is more likely, convinced that she was a runaway; she was never mentioned. At this time, the two other suspects were discarded. While Olson's name had come up in the Weller investigation, a mis-remembered date had given him an alibi and, in any event, Richmond RCMP still had another 'very promising suspect' who was later to be exonerated.

On July 19, two Surrey youths were arrested and charged with extortion for demanding a ransom from the Partington family. When questioned, the youths obviously knew nothing at all of Simon's whereabouts. It was the kind of cruel thing a youthful Olson might have done.

On July 20, *The Province* carried a story on the Highway Murders, a series of eleven unsolved murders along the Trans-Canada and Yellowhead Highways since 1973. One slaying had taken place near Edmonton, four near Calgary and six in the B.C. Interior. The latest victim had been found on May 8 near Kamloops; the previous on February 28 west of Golden. All the victims were women of a similar stocky build and had long auburn or reddish hair. Most of them had been raped and some had been sexually mutilated. Some had been stabbed numerous times, others had been strangled by hand or garotted and some had been struck repeatedly with rocks or a blunt instrument. The Kamloops RCMP had a 763-page file on these murders and was appealing for leads. The feeling of uneasiness spread.

On July 22, Olson was charged with indecent assault for the attack of July 7. He had just returned from California.

On Thursday, July 23, Raymond King Jr., 15, disappeared from New Westminster before noon. His bike was found chained up near the Canada Manpower Centre, where he had gone to look for work. He had decided to stay with his father while his mother went East that summer.

Much later that evening, Joan Olson answered the doorbell and let Dennis Tarr into their apartment. Cliff, she said was 'taking a shower.' Tarr and Olson discussed his becoming a police informant. The items of interest ranged from information on stolen property, armed robberies, break-ins, drug offences, and, if necessary, "...bigger and heavier things, like homicides."

Olson said that he didn't know if he could give Tarr any information on murders. Talk turned to the large prominently displayed bible resting on the coffee table. Tarr got the impression that Olson was reasonably familiar with it.

Olson picked up a newspaper with a story about Simon Partington and speculated that there were three reasons behind his disappearance; ransom, which he dismissed by saying the family didn't seem to have much money; a hit and run accident, in which the driver had stopped and taken the body away to hide elsewhere; and, finally, that Simon might have been picked up by "some pervert."

Olson was very critical of the reliability of the witness who'd seen Simon with the muscular blonde man: speaking of tans, he showed Tarr his own well-developed tan, explaining that they had just returned from Knott's Berry Farm in California. Patiently, Tarr mentioned that he'd taken his family there as well, trying hard to build rapport. They agreed to meet again two days later in Surrey.

While this meeting was under way, RCMP investigators were discussing the implementation of surveillance with District Headquarters; however, no commitment was made due to "...a lack of manpower to supplement the specialized surveillance team."

On July 24, the Partington rewards totalled $6,500.

Burnaby RCMP asked the Co-ordinated Law Enforcement Unit (CLEU) for help. Before it could be granted, "...additional profile information and a contingency plan had to be drawn up."

On July 25, Judy Kozma's body was found in Weaver Creek Provincial Park near Harrison Mills.

On that same day, Sigrun Arnd, 18, a tourist from West Germany, disappeared. No one noticed immediately, because although she was known to be travelling through the States toward Vancouver, she was only vaguely expected to arrive here about the end of July. Carelessly, Olson had been seen with her in a Coquitlam pub and the pair were later seen again on a dike by the passengers of a passing train. He had taken about $200 in traveller's cheques from Arnd.

On July 27, Terri Lyn Carson, 15, disappeared after going to Guildford to apply for a pet shop job. She had known Christine Weller; Weller had once lived in Carson's Surrey apartment building at 136th St. and 10th Ave.

When he had hidden Carson's body in the vicinity of Court's near Agassiz, Olson drove to Hope and cashed Arnd's traveller's cheques, signing them with some fictitious name. It wasn't even a serious attempt at forgery, something in which Olson used to take pride. Surprisingly, he got away with it. It is possible that, if challenged, he was prepared to use false documents to prove his identity; he could use them once and throw them away. His ability to charm people with glib talk probably diverted the cashier's attention just enough to make the scam work.

Mrs. Carson thought that it was just possible that Terri Lyn had run away, especially since a girl matching her description was seen at the Turf Hotel several times in the next two weeks. The sightings had helped to convince the Surrey RCMP that she was a runaway. The RCMP in general seems to have made biased value judgments of the victim's families, believing that if a child came from a single-parent home, the child was a runaway and not a potential victim.

Far too late in the day to save Terri Lyn Carson, The Special 'O' Squad began tailing Olson at 4:45 pm on July 27.

On July 28, Tarr and Olson met in the parking lot of the Cariboo Road Hotel in Coquitlam. Tarr told Olson that police would be very interested in help in locating any of the several missing youngsters. After talking about where in the Lower Mainland the children might be found, there was a moment of silence. "I'm going to give you something that will make you a lieutenant," Olson said. "I don't want to be a lieutenant." Tarr replied, trying to appear distant and composed. "Pick a number between one and ten." said Olson. "Nine," said Tarr, feeling that Olson wanted him to say 'nine;' it was the number of children then missing.

Olson was grinning; for someone who had spent so much time in jail, he always seemed awfully cheerful. "I'll tell you what," he said, "I'll give you a letter and in it there'll be nine numbers, each corresponding to a location. What you find there will be your own business." He went on to say that he didn't want to testify about what might be found at those locations, nor did he want police calling at his apartment. Almost hesitantly, Olson asked Tarr to get him on the payroll as an informant. Tarr said he'd look into it.

Overnight on July 28 - 29, the surveillance ended, as the Special 'O' squad became convinced that Olson had realized that he was being followed. They had arrested him and two other men when they picked up two teen-aged girls in Surrey. By 3:30 am, Olson was on the move once again.

On July 29, Detective Larry Gaudette of the New Westminster Police decided to meet with Burnaby and Surrey RCMP to see if the Court, Partington and King cases could be related. Kozma was still considered a runaway.

On July 30, Tarr, surreptitiously wearing a tape recorder, met Olson and a youth in the Surrey Inn coffee shop. For nearly three-quarters of an hour, their discussion centred on various minor crimes, especially armed robberies, in the Lower Mainland. At one point, Olson mentioned that he and another youth had shared some beer with a couple of teen-aged girls whom they had picked up two days earlier and that they were later stopped by police. This incident, which Olson seems to have taken in stride, is what made the RCMP drop the surveillance. The question is whether Olson read it as a 'tail' or as an everyday occurrence for him – no one knew for sure.

Tarr and Olson dropped the youth off and continued on to the White Spot on Scott Road where they met Cpl. Fred Maile of the Serious Crime Section. Maile was wearing a wire and another Mountie eavesdropped and taped the conversation from his car. The conversation, much of which was general and repetitious, lasted for thirty minutes. Maile pressed Olson for something to prove the value of his allusions and Olson again asked to be put on the payroll as an informant at $3,000 a month.

The Serious Crime Section of the Vancouver RCMP detachment had been formed in 1977 to assist in the investigations involving many detachments. Its predecessors were special investigation units formed on two previous occasions in the past ten years; these were a series of six sex slayings of women around B.C. between 1969 and 1974, for which a suspected was charged and convicted in the States, and again in 1976, when it was unsuccessful in solving the murders of twelve women. Directed by Insp. Larry Proke, a twenty-three year veteran, it consisted of 10 men and had access to sophisticated techniques for everything from surveillance to forensic identification.

Olson suggested that he might be able to get information on some important local criminals. He reminded them of how useful he'd been in the 1976 Gary Marcoux case. Marcoux, accused of raping and murdering a 10-year old girl near Mission, had been in the cell next to Olson's in Oakalla. Olson gained his confidence to the point that Marcoux wrote him a letter confessing to the murder. Olson promptly snitched on Marcoux, who was sentenced to life.

Maile confirmed that there was cash available for information, especially if it related to several unsolved murders. "The rewards range from $5,000 to more than $100,000 for one case." he told Olson. Olson was interested but he repeated that he did not want to be required to testify. He had been stabbed seven times by Gordon Lussier in a 1976 attack in Prince Albert after Olson had ratted on his friends. The attack earned Lussier an extra six years and netted Olson $3500 and a commendation for bravery from the Saskatchewan Criminal Compensation Board. Olson had been in the high-maximum security Saskatchewan Pen four times; he had escaped from it twice in 1968.

On Thursday, July 30, Louise Chartrand, 17, disappeared while en route to her job as a waitress in Maple Ridge. Maple Ridge RCMP did not link her disappearance to those of the other missing young people. As any teenager does, she'd had a recent argument with her mother and had even talked to friends about leaving home.

On the same day, Judy Kozma's nude body was found in Weaver Creek Provincial Park near Harrison Mills; police did not release this fact until the next day. "But there's no direct evidence to indicate...the cases are directly linked," said Cpl. Les Forsythe of the Burnaby RCMP.

On July 30, Supt. Bruce Northorp took command of the entire operation; there were nearly 150 men concentrating on the disappearances. Northorp was a 33-year veteran, having begun his police career with the B.C. Provincial Police; his long-planned retirement was just a few months away – this would be his last case.

On July 31, when the Special 'O' surveillance squad was brought in, they discovered that Olson was missing; he'd slipped away to Calgary.

Special 'O,' The Special Observation Section, consisted primarily of ten men drawn from the RCMP and the Co-ordinated Law Enforcement Unit (CLEU), a Vancouver-based police group that specialized in intelligence-gathering and the investigation of organized crime and major offences. Their techniques and hardware included multiple-car tails, in which the suspect is alternately observed by cars ahead of him and behind him, 'bumper beepers,' which are electronic location indicators, as well as cameras and tape recorders.

On August 2, Sandor Kozma, who had learned from TV news, not the police, how his daughter had died, publicly voiced his criticism: "The police initially appeared to treat her disappearance as a routine missing-person case." Kozma should have been dealt with better, but generally, victim's families do not understand why they are not told more about the case. Good police procedures dictate the minimum release of information at all times.

On August 5, the body of Raymond King Jr. was found near the northern edge of Weaver Creek Provincial Park.

King's body was found approximately 1.5 kilometres from where Judy Kozma had been found the previous week. A hiker had alerted police to 'a bad smell' and the dog had completed the task. The RCMP considered using divers to search Weaver Lake and helicopters to search the adjacent bush. The ground forces consisted of four dogs and a dog-master from Burnaby and approximately 30 men from the Agassiz detachment and the Serious Crime Section.

On August 6, having just returned from Calgary, Olson phoned Tarr. They talked about the discovery of King's body the day before and agreed to meet after church on Sunday August 9. Olson was adamant about the police having money ready for information. The 'Special O' squad began following Olson again; in the next few days, they witnessed him commit a burglary in Burnaby, but took no action; he was now a murder suspect. The tail continued.

The 'Find Verna Fund' then stood at $3000. Local volunteers had been searching the steep, desolate side-roads of the Yale-Hope area with four-wheel drive vehicles. False leads and sightings had come from as far away as Billings, Montana and Winnipeg.

On August 7, Chris Burgess, a King family friend, said that he intended to continue with a public appeal to find the killer. Burgess called on Ottawa to set up a task force to co-ordinate the search efforts. "This is getting to be a matter of national urgency. We are obviously dealing with a psychotic." Burgess described King Sr.'s anger over RCMP delays in verifying that they had found his son's body. On the 6th, as soon as King Sr. had been told that a male body had been found, he made his son's dental records available to the RCMP: he still had not yet received official notification that the body was that of Raymond Jr. Burgess's point was that dental checks could be done conclusively in about 30 minutes; (this is reasonable if, all the teeth are recovered intact and enough distinctive dental work had been done) it was now more than 24 hours since they records had been released. Burgess, whose amateur efforts were often very annoying, said he believed that police were not co-operating with each other. "They don't like to work in unison. They've been moving on this like a snail on Valium." Chilliwack RCMP later said that they still didn't have King Jr.'s dental records, so the examination hadn't been made.

On the same day, Insp. Proke said that one, then later, three computers were being used to analyze the case evidence. "We are setting up a program to ..."; setting up meant that they did not, at that time, have a functioning, proven program to do what they claimed was being done. Such a program, called an expert system, was hardly known to exist in academic circles at the time. They are best suited to factual, rule-driven situations, like engineering design.

The RCMP had now asked taxi companies, transit and trucking firms to urge their drivers to report anything suspicious. Finally, a formal warning was issued to parents to advise their children to avoid strangers at all times and not to hitch-hike.

On August 9, Olson did not show up and Tarr never got the promised letter Olson had been so smug about.

On August 11, Gail Smith, Collen Daignault's aunt and legal guardian, deeply embarrassed Insp. Proke by publicly criticizing the Surrey RCMP for "...treating her disappearance just like another runaway. But I know she didn't run away – I've told them that constantly." Smith complained that she hadn't been told that the special investigators were even aware of Colleen's case. Proke said that he wasn't aware of it; Surrey RCMP refused to comment.

Grace McCarthy, whose B.C. Human Resources Ministry was responsible for thousands of children, suggested that the Lower Mainland had "its own little Atlanta going on," in a reference to the slayings of black men in Georgia, and announced that she would ask the provincial government to post a reward to help solve the child-killing cases.

On August 12, Attorney-General Allan Williams tried to cool the frenzy, saying that a reward would only hamper the investigation.

On August 12, 'Special O' officers stopped Olson's rented van near Ucluelet on Vancouver Island. They had followed him for some time after he had picked up two female hitchhikers, who were never identified publicly. Olson was charged with two drunken driving offences but almost immediately, plans were made to fly him back to the Mainland. In searching the van, RCMP found Judy Kozma's name and phone number in an address book. It was suspicious, but it was insufficient to base a conviction on.

In West Vancouver, a memorial service was held for Raymond King Jr. In addition to his own family and friends, the families and friends of some of the other missing children also attended. Outside, the RCMP noted down the licence numbers of all cars for blocks around the church. In its acceleratingly desperate search for clues, as the mourners filed out, the RCMP openly photographed the entire group.

Chris Burgess announced the start of a fund-raising drive to finance the printing of posters, general advertising and the three private investigators working for the families. These men donated their time and received only expenses.

The following day, August 13, John Hall, a defence lawyer respected for his courtroom skills and his calm attitude, was asked to serve as the special prosecutor in the case. In contrast to the American District Attorney, who is commonly an elected official and is so often seen on TV, the Canadian Crown Counsel or prosecutor, who is appointed to the position (it is a job offer few refuse) is seldom involved in a case before the police present him with their compiled evidence and a request that formal charges be laid. It can be done either way in Canada. Hall was then available to advise the RCMP during the rest of their investigation.

Olson was flown back from Vancouver Island and delivered to the Burnaby RCMP. The official toll stood at three dead and five missing.

The Partington reward was now $8000, as the result of donations by his father's employer and union brothers, churches and private individuals. Mrs. King's employer had pledged $5000, asking that it be applied to recovering information relating to any of the disappearances.

The RCMP had now broadened its appeal for information to CB radio clubs, taxi, bus and truck drivers, motorists and the general public.

On August 14, Clifford Olson was arraigned in Burnaby Provincial Court and charged with the two drunken driving offences; Hall had some aces up his sleeve to keep Olson in custody for some time – separate breakings and enterings on Rumble St. on August 7 and on Norland Ave. on August 12 plus several outstanding earlier charges, mostly sexual in nature that had neither been stayed or pressed. In all likelihood, Olson was softened up (disoriented) by being kept in a windowless, clockless cell whose lights were never dimmed; by being served three identical meals each day, say, three breakfasts; and by never being allowed to sleep – someone would pop into his cell every few minutes "...just to see if you're okay..." The courtroom was full of reporters, artists and the curious.

On August 18th, Olson suggested that he could direct the police to the bodies if, and only if, his wife received some financial reward. RCMP discussed it with John Hall, who felt that without substantially more evidence, it was problematical whether he could even secure a conviction in the Kozma case – all the others were even shakier. There was great concern that Olson was trying to fabricate some sort of insanity defence and thus beat the rap on the Kozma case. At one point, Olson had talked alarmingly of selling the information to the media and the victim's families. Hall felt that it would not hinder his prosecution of the case. Nor did he ever feel that any of Olson's statements were inadmissible as evidence.

In whatever manner the bargaining was conducted, it was eventually agreed that Olson would receive $30,000 for information leading to the location of four bodies and an additional $10,000 per body for the locations of another six bodies. Attorney-General Allan Williams gave his approval.

On the 18th, Insp. Proke was still complaining that the current spell of warm weather was hindering the use of infrared scanners to find the bodies; the numerous rocks around Weaver Creek, he said, cooled down so slowly that they 'jumbled' the scanner readings. It is impossible to use infrared scanners for this purpose. If the RCMP did attempt this, it was due to their desperation and the aggressiveness of scanner salesmen of the day. Of course, it may have been a red herring to placate the press, the public and the victim's families. They were also still clinging to the idea that Weller and Carson did "...not fit the pattern," and Supt. Northorp said that Carson was "...not on the list, but we are aware of her."

On August 19, Terri Lyn Carson and Colleen Daignault were officially added to the list of victims.

On August 20, Olson agreed to the arranged offer of cash for bodies. Suddenly, no one who had been a party to the negotiations wanted to have any further part of it, so a local lawyer was hired as a trust intermediary to receive and transfer the money to Mrs. Olson.

Chris Burgess, whose well-meaning efforts to publicize the disappearances had earned him the nickname

'Sherlock,' announced that he was launching a group entitled Children In Distressing Situations, (CIDS) expressed doubt that the RCMP had found the murderer of all the missing children. He said that the private investigators would continue to work for the victim's families.

On August 21, Olson, described as a self-employed construction worker, appeared in Chilliwack Provincial Court and was charged with the murder of Judy Kozma. This was the only case for which any reasonable evidence existed at that time; the RCMP knew they had four other murdered children but they still thought the remainder were runaways. The hearing was interrupted for an hour and a half while a local doctor examined Olson's mental condition. He reported that he might be suffering from some form of mental illness and recommended that a psychiatric assessment be completed before proceeding. The judge ordered a 30-day remand for that purpose.

Newspapers, TV news and especially open-line radio broadcasts spoke of little else for weeks. The public found it impossible to grasp that one human being could have behaved in such a manner. It was the worst of times.

On August 24, the RCMP requested permission to complete the cash for bodies deal; Deputy Commissioner Henry Jensen sent authorization from Ottawa the next day. The remainder of the month of August was taken up with the recovery of the bodies. Olson was secretly taken from Oakalla and driven to whichever location his fancy selected. Once there, he gave some directions to the police and assembled workmen, and stood back, calm, composed, occasionally almost smiling, visibly enjoying his little outing. Hall felt that only the murderer or an accomplice could have known where the bodies were located and that his case was now considerably strengthened.

On August 31, Olson was charged with eight additional counts of first-degree murder.

On September 10, RCMP Commissioner Robert Simmonds and Solicitor-General Robert Kaplan were finally informed that the deal had been made.

Sometime early in September, Paddy Sherman, the publisher of *The Province,* had a visit from Attorney-General Allan Williams. Williams had two concerns; first, he was certain that *Province* reporters had found out more than the paper had published, meaning the payment deal, (Sherman agreed with him, confirming later that his reporters were aware of it) and lastly, he wanted to maintain an environment in which Olson could be expected to receive a fair trial. Sherman replied that *The Province* had already voluntarily refrained from printing items that would have prejudiced the trial.

Williams never asked Sherman not to print any specific items and both agreed that when the story was made public after the trial, Sherman could tell the public of the meeting.

Various other media executives agreed to the call for silence. However, Clark Davey, publisher of *The Sun,* told Williams that the whole thing was "a crock" and that while his paper would not break the silence, that he was completely opposed to the deal and the tacit request for self-censorship.

On September 21, another charge of first-degree murder was laid, bringing the number to ten.

On October 16, Elmer MacKay (Conservative, Central Nova) asked Kaplan in the House whether he was "...aware of any circumstances whereby the RCMP or their agents pay, or expedite the payment of money to accused persons or their families, in trust or otherwise, for the purpose of obtaining evidence relevant to the offence with which an accused is charged." He specifically cited Olson. Kaplan said he couldn't comment on a case before the courts, but added that neither he nor anyone in his ministry had tried "...to suppress or influence the press in any way..." Mackay's Nova Scotia riding had seen a recent brutal child murder by another convict released under mandatory supervision.

On October 28, Attorney-General Williams signed a direct indictment against Olson, moving the case past a preliminary hearing towards trial in January of 1982.

On October 29, MacKay, in a continuing criticism of mandatory supervision, alleged that in Olson's case, the community assessment report was ignored. Kaplan, citing human unpredictability, responded with truisms and cliches, and promised to look into the matter.

On November 30, Mackay returned to the attack. He quoted 'an eminent sociologist,' whose name was not read into the record, as saying, "...the Solicitor-General and his staff are quite wrong in assuming that dangerousness cannot be predicted." MacKay did "...not believe that there was co-ordination between the penal and parole institutions and the prison authorities and the police forces."

Jim Peterson, Parliamentary Secretary to the Minister of Justice, who was then Jean Chretien, defended mandatory supervision. He said only 25% of inmates so released are convicted of a new offence while under supervision, and only about 6% are convicted of violent crimes. He closed by saying, "We are not happy with this particular process. That is why the Solicitor-General has undertaken the study, the results of which should be known soon, and he will be acting on it."

On January 10, 1982, Olson entered a plea of not guilty before Mr. Justice Harry McKay in B.C. Supreme Court. Olson was to be defended by Robert Shantz and Michael Rhodes, while the Prosecution consisted of John Hall, assisted by Sandra Cunningham. The fiery, down-to-earth Shantz, with his salt-and-pepper beard, contrasted sharply with the unflappable, clean-shaven Hall.

Jury selection began from a list of 140 people taken from a recent voters list. Of these, eleven were excluded due to medical or family reasons and five others declared that their impartiality had been prejudiced by radio, TV and newspaper accounts of the case. Shantz disqualified 11 middle-aged women in using 19 of his 20 allowable challenges of jurors. Finally, a selection of seven men and five women was settled upon.

The jurors, whose duty might last from four to eight weeks, would be paid $20.00 per day for the first ten days and $30.00 per day thereafter. There is both a personal and a public cost to seeing justice served. The jury was promptly sequestered in a downtown hotel at the Crown's expense in order to shield them from any further media coverage of the trial. The trial's cost was estimated to be as high as $250,000.

After the plea was entered, the jury was removed to permit a *voir dire* to be held. A *voir dire* – literally, 'to see and to speak,' is a trial within a trial to determine the admissibility of controversial evidence before it may actually be presented by the Prosecution. Here, it was the tape-recorded evidence that was of concern and it was expected to require about two weeks to decide it. The jury would hear none of the tapes until their admissibility was settled. The process of a *voir dire* may not be reported by the media. Surprisingly, at the end of the *voir dire*, Judge McKay ruled it could be reported, since the jury had been sequestered.

Tactically, Hall faced a particular problem in proving first-degree murder. The deaths must be shown to be planned and deliberate, and since the bodies were in advanced states of decay, it was impossible to prove that Olson had sexually assaulted any of them. In countless hours of interrogation, Olson had said much under both 'warned' and 'unwarned' conditions; he had talked of body counts far in excess of the ten for which he was being tried; he had frustratingly manouevred back and forth between the first and third person in his conversations, speaking often of "my friend," much in the way a child talks of an imaginary playmate, but he was very careful never to say anything about sexual assault nor that the murders were anything but spontaneous incidents.

In his January 13th testimony, Dennis Tarr described his meetings with Olson and the surreptitious tapes were played. As the morning drew towards its close, it probably became clear to Olson that Hall was going to introduce as evidence every grisly travesty that he had committed on each of his victims; Olson had a lot to think about over lunch. Do not mistake his reaction as remorse; Olson could switch moods and roles disconcertingly quickly – he merely wanted to cast himself in the 'best' possible light. And it rankled him that people would know him as he really was.

Upon re-entering the courtroom after lunch, Olson attempted to speak directly to Hall. He was led away by Sheriffs and Judge McKay ordered him to take his seat in the prisoner's dock. Olson and Shantz then spoke for perhaps thirty seconds before Shantz asked Judge McKay for a meeting in chambers.

After some fifteen minutes recess, they re-appeared and Shantz asked for a postponement until the next morning so that he might obtain written instructions relating to disposition. Olson was a difficult client for any lawyer and had already told police things that could hinder any defence his lawyer might present. Whether this postponement meant a change in plea, a change in defence strategy, or even a change in defence counsel or that Shantz foresaw problems in accepting or challenging Crown evidence or something else entirely was open to speculation.

On January 14, Olson entered the courtroom looking decidedly down, in contrast to his usual cheerful appearance, facade though it may have been. After the call to order, Shantz rose and said, "M'lord, I am instructed to seek a reversal of the plea. He intends to plead guilty to all the counts."

Judge McKay questioned Shantz and Olson briefly on a point of evidence and to determine whether Olson understood the implications of the new plea, and satisfied that Olson did understand, he instructed the clerk to read the charges to the prisoner. Olson was required to say 'guilty' at the end of each charge. The Crown now entered a similar charge in the case of Sandra Wolfsteiner, so in the end, Olson was charged with eleven murders. Judge McKay then addressed the jury, telling them that they could "take the matter as proven." and sent them out to consider their verdict. They returned quickly with their verdict; it was guilty. Court was a little more than half an hour into its day and it was over.

"I do not have the words to adequately describe the enormity of your crimes or to adequately describe the heartbreak and anguish you have brought to so many people," said Justice McKay, in sentencing Clifford Robert

Olson Jr. to concurrent life imprisonment on each of eleven counts. He recommended that, the Criminal Code provisions of parole eligibility after twenty-five years notwithstanding, that parole should never be granted to him. "It would be foolhardy to have you at large."

So ended the first known instance of a criminal being paid for information on his own crimes.

With the eleventh and last 'guilty,' Olson had broken the silence. Within minutes of sentencing, Hall confirmed from the Courthouse steps that the money had been paid out, ending the worst-kept secret of the trial. Many reporters knew of it, as they had known of other bits of evidence much earlier, but all had held their silence so as not to jeopardize the investigation and to ensure the atmosphere of a fair trial. Their desire to see justice done, not fear of contempt of court charges, had kept them silent.

In the new furore over the deal, Kaplan, RCMP Commissioner Simmonds and Prime Minister Trudeau defended it as distasteful but needful. Trudeau compared it to journalists paying criminals for the exclusive rights to their stories, noting that the public has come to accept the police paying informants for crime leads.

Trudeau said that he, as a parent, felt much better with Olson in jail, rather than merely "still a suspect but still free to go around and be in a position where he could murder other children in British Columbia."

Allan Williams made the mistake of his career by denying that the deal had been made until reporters embarrassed him into recanting. Dave Barrett, the New Democratic opposition leader, called for a full public enquiry into the matter, saying that the government had a responsibility to ensure that there was no public unrest about its handling. He feared, as did many others, that it might prompt others to copy it in some way in order to profit from crime.

The disappearance of Verna Bjerky was never solved and, in the end, was not attributed to Olson. Various sources estimate that Olson may have killed as many as 40 young people; he later said he had begun killing in the 60s while in the States. He has long since ceased to be co-operative and little of what he says is likely to be truthful, however tantalizing it may sound.

We need follow the story no further in detail. It is still a controversial topic almost fourteen years after the first disappearance. In ways both large and small, the loss and the grieving continues – and may never end – for the families of the victims.

It was the worst of times.

Bear in mind that I was just a couple of weeks from retirement when the case began to unfold and that it was, with the exception of the New Westminster police and Dennis Tarr, strictly an RCMP operation: while everyone was curious, very few were privileged enough to hear anything significant.

In terms of 1982 dollars, it was estimated that Olson's twenty-five year minimum sentence would cost the taxpayers approximately $1,025,000; annual per capita costs have since risen from the relatively modest $41,000, so the estimate was way too low. In 1992 - 93, it cost $69,288 to maintain an inmate in a maximum-security institution.

After the 30-day appeal period expired, Olson was transferred to Kingston Penitentiary, where he remained until near the end of 1992, when he was moved to the Saskatchewan Penitentiary in Prince Albert, which is a high-maximum security institution. Olson much prefers it to Kingston; his cell has a window and the food is far better.

Much about Olson is paradoxical: that he was sexually-abused when four, he dismisses as '...no big deal, the sort of thing all kids go through.'; that, in prison, he does not fit the usual inmate pattern, carrying himself with a poise far different from the usual convict's bravado strut or hang-dog shuffle; that, if he killed for the first time in 1980 at the age of forty-one, he was the only known serial killer to begin killing after turning twenty; that in a career said to total 103 convictions, none of these offences was of a sexual nature.

There were four patterns which emerged in the investigation, and none of them was significant in unravelling it: four victims had disappeared on Thursdays; four were connected, as tenants or as visitors, to the four apartment buildings; and their bodies were found in clusters, 3 in Richmond, 3 near Harrison Mills and 2 near Agassiz; fair complexions and blondish hair were predominant amongst the victims. What was uncharacteristic of a serial killer was the mixture of male and female victims and the variety of means by which they were slain. What might have followed next is anybody's guess.

In Olson's own estimation, not being charged with a crime or being acquitted of it is the same as being totally and unconditionally innocent. Can you imagine trying get at his record under the Freedom of Information Act? Again, the 'expert' at that sort of manipulation of the system is Olson himself. He began his dogged study of the law with the old Deifenbaker Bill of Rights, but he prefers working with the Charter of Rights and Freedoms.

Since his conviction in 1982, Olson has sent some twenty cases to the Supreme Court of Canada and lost them all; he has become an expert in using the Charter to keep the government and the courts busy fending off his challenges; very few powerful, well-trained lawyers will ever be able to boast of such legal one-upmanship. These have all been, and will continue to be, nuisance actions, with no relation to his principal conviction or sentence.

As he grew up in Richmond, Olson certainly exhibited anti-social behaviour yet it was crime for profit, not bullying, which characterized his youth. Everyone considered him a nuisance rather than a menace. The 1957 report accompanying his first conviction for breaking and entering at the age of seventeen attributed him a 'dull normal IQ,' that is, below 100, when 98 to 114 is considered normal. He barely finished Grade 8, but he's had a lot of time to read since then, and he has since earned marks in the eighties and nineties in correspondence courses from Queen's University in Kingston. Queen's markers don't seem to place too much emphasis on language skills; what little has been made public of Olson's writings displays juvenile sentence structure, modest grammar, chronic malapropisms and spelling that hints at dyslexia.

I am stunned that such a person could have eluded those provisions of the Criminal Code which pertain to dangerous offenders; the earlier term was 'habitual criminal.' On first glance, Olson would seem to have qualified easily by 1974. Had such an action been taken against Olson, it is most likely that his crimes of 1980 – 81 would not, indeed, could not have been committed.

He has, however, forced prison officials to apologize for describing him as a sexual offender; technically, he is not, because he was only charged with murder, not rape or sexual assault, and none of his previous sex-related charges were pressed and proven. This curious action by the Crown may have been necessitated by the decomposed state of the bodies, which would have precluded finding any evidence of sexual activity.

In the last half of the Twentieth Century, it is very difficult, at least in North America and Europe, for a person to reach maturity without encountering bureaucracy in the form of teachers, employers and the police, some of whom should be able to detect some symptoms of abnormal behaviour. Very few serial killers leap full-blown onto the public scene; they have been building up to it for some years. They have, by necessity, been understudies to numerous others, many of whom may remain minor criminals but they were unwittingly childhood idols, models and mentors to the monster now ready to emerge. Andy Warhol said, "Each of us is famous for fifteen minutes." Was he correct? Is that part of what motivates serial killers?

Along the way, police, prosecutors, prison guards, parole officers, social workers and others recognized him as a manipulative liar with strong egocentric tendencies and a bad parole risk, yet they describe him as 'nonviolent and harmless.' Was he hiding his true nature? There is little or no evidence that he is that clever, but the answer will likely never be known. Or did his mind suddenly undergo some change of state? Several psychiatric examiners concluded unanimously that he was fit to stand trial, but even if a person is legally sane, the possibility of horrific aberrant behaviour cannot be ruled out. The question of his mental state will, in all probability, never be settled.

One characteristics displayed by some serial killers is the ability to ingratiate themselves with their victims by charming and persuasive conversation; Ted Bundy, who looked like 'the boy next door,' and Olson, who certainly did not when the murders occurred, were both particularly good at this. But Olson despised Bundy because, in his opinion, Bundy killed only for sex…but Olson still envied him his publicity and notoriety.

I keep wondering if Olson planned the entire operation from the outset, right down to the last detail. Much is made of his supposedly marginal IQ, but such tests have been criticized for their built-in biases for decades. It seems to me that he could have decided, using whatever twisted logic, that the only way to provide adequately for his wife and son in the long term was to make a huge 'score' in such a way that the loot was unrecoverable but yet available to them in his absence. That meant cash and some sure-fire transfer method. The Olson's have since divorced; whatever the reasons, it places a further barrier between the cash and the many people who urged that it be somehow recovered.

In prison, Olson has become a Roman Catholic, whether his conversion is genuine or not, he now believes that "…God has forgiven me, and that's all there is to say."

Olson is once again in Prince Albert, in a prison from which he has escaped twice in the past, albeit not from such secure quarters, and he claims to be 'enjoying himself.'

As this book was nearing completion, Olson once again made the news. The victim of his assault on January 1, 1981, came forward in Calgary to press her story once again. The trauma and guilt she has suffered for thirteen years as Olson's only surviving victim don't belong to her, she said, but to those in the system who disbelieved her and permitted Olson to go free and to kill another ten children. That Cpl. Jim Hunter, who investigated her claim then and still believes her, gives added strength to her assessment.

Attorney-General Colin Gabelmann has asked Bob Wright, B.C.'s chief Crown prosecutor, for a full report on the case. In the House of Commons, Justice Minister Allan Rock, speaking for the absent Solicitor-General Herb Gray, said that he was sure that "...the Solicitor-General will want to consider the matter and inquire to determine the facts." Perhaps the inquiries that were so firmly refused in 1982 will now be conducted.

You will, of course, have formed your own opinions about this case. Hindsight allows us to see what should have been done, and we see that it is very different from what was done.

Did the penal system, which likes to style itself 'correctional,' fail to detect his symptoms and treat Olson accordingly? Was it, as a penal system, ever intended to 'treat' rather than 'punish?' – try shadow-boxing with that for a while.

Did the RCMP fail in various ways to respond quickly and realistically to the disappearances? Admittedly, that is hard to answer, but their continued insistence that so many cases were unrelated probably prolonged the process and led to more deaths. Paranoia is an awful affliction, but in such cases, police ought to ask themselves whether they are paranoid enough; a more suspicious attitude on their part might have led them to Olson sooner. Of all the officers and men involved, Les Forsythe did the best job – what he was trained to do – without any concern about appearances or political repercussions. Others, such as Jim Hunter, Fred Maile and Dennis Tarr, played strong supporting parts. All police forces could use more members like these men.

The role of some Crown prosecutors needs to be looked at closely. Not only must the question of dismissing the New Year's Day assault be dealt with, but the other numerous charges which Olson accumulated without causing any significant response from the Crown should be clarified. The habitual criminal issue was noted earlier.

And what of the politicians? It was they who contrived the overlapping jurisdictions that led to inter-service and even inter-detachment rivalries which helped to obscure the overall picture. It was they who repeatedly assured the public that no inquiries were needed; they deserved more trouble than they got. Remember, politicians are relatively easy to change; you just need a long enough memory of enough outrageous nonsense.

Society will, statistically, continue to produce occasional individuals who exhibit such aberrant behaviour. What society seems unable to do – or perhaps it is financially unwilling to do? – is to recognize such latent behaviour and combat it either with treatment or with another response which will protect the innocent majority.

It was the worst of times.

Epilogue

I retired from the Vancouver City Police on September 1, 1981, with the rank of Detective, which I had held for seventeen years.

In 1968, it had taken only one recently-promoted Superintendent, who has since died, to say, "We don't need experts; any detective can handle this work." to initiate crippling changes to our efficient Morality Squad of four detectives and one sergeant. All of our files were destroyed. The mugshot book was discarded. The rapists and molesters had a field day. Oh, if only the public knew then what I'm telling you now!

I was transferred to the Fraudulent Cheque Squad, whose Sergeant had also been ordered to destroy their suspect files, but he merely kept them without comment – or incident – and they helped us to put many people in jail.

During one of the major rape cases following this change, I asked the Superintendent how the 'crystal ball' system was working: I could never keep my mouth shut.

The Parole Board hasn't improved much over the years either. The recent cases of Danny Perrault and Jason Gamache emphasize the uncertainties of assessing the state of the criminal mind—and the insanity of blithely paroling criminals with a record of vicious, antisocial behaviour. Gamache could almost be a clone of Garry Head, except that his crime lacked Head's revenge motive—it had no motive save self-gratification through terrorizing and murdering a child.

It does absolutely no good for Dave Bahr, Correctional Service Canada's B.C. Regional Director, to say that he felt just sick about the whole (Gamache) affair and wished it could be undone; "We goofed terribly." Yes, but will you ever learn? The public doesn't see much progress there.

Every change in the law during the past several years has been to the advantage of the criminals. The justice system seems unconcerned about the victims. The Supreme Court of Canada moves in step with all the decisions of the U.S. Supreme Court. Most of its decisions seem to protect the criminals at expense of their victims.

I believe that we need a return to capital punishment; some members of our society are not fit to live amongst those of us who are peaceable and law-abiding. We do not allow rabid dogs to roam freely, and that is exactly what serial killers are—rabid dogs.

On a more positive note, I can tell you that Garry Head is still in prison for the murder of Tanya Busch, so the system hasn't failed us completely. Maybe if more of us told our MLAs and MPs what we wanted, or even got ourselves organized, we'd see the improvements that we want.

The Vancouver City Police Force has re-established a specialized Morality Squad, and it's highly-trained detectives are doing a fine job. Every Force occasionally suffers under well-meaning but inadequate management practices. As of 1994, I believe that it is second to none in Canada.

It must be remembered that an investigator's purpose is to protect the innocent. There is no room for error. The rapid improvements in DNA matching from minute samples of bodily tissue will result in it's recognition as a means of positive identification equal or superior to fingerprints. As it becomes harder and harder to avoid detection, the criminals respond by becoming more sophisticated and enlisting the aid of their own scientific experts. Though courts are currently reluctant to admit some kinds of scientific evidence as foolproof, juries no doubt have greater faith in science now than they have ever had in the past. The most important part of the process still involves convincing human beings that the accused is guilty.

The greatest aid to investigators is the Canadian Police Information Centre (CPIC); it stores and sorts all pertinent information on criminals and suspects in a database which is available to all police forces in Canada.

Mobile radios and cellular phones, in the hands of both police and citizens, are making it harder for criminals to avoid detection and capture. In the old days, foot patrols had to find and use a call box to report anything.

Auld Lang Syne

When Don Winterton became Chief, he offered Nick Lohin a Sergeantcy and said that he'd see that Nick became an Inspector in short order. He made the same offer to me, but Nick went and I stayed. Those who got behind Winterton went up the ladder quickly. Winterton could talk well and promoted Community Policing. It all sounded pretty neat but it wasn't much different than the old-fashioned idea of walking a beat, which still has a lot to recommend it.

Many friends and colleagues became chiefs: Bill Snowden in Victoria, Ken Brown in New Westminster, Joe Hornell in West Vancouver, Doug McLeod in Delta, Irvin Bailey in Oak Bay and George Moore became Deputy Chief in Saskatoon. Winterton and I had worked together on several occasions as Detectives, and Bob Stewart, whom Winterton chose as his successor, had been a Morality Detective with me.

Our Detective Office Secretary, June Martin, who is still on the job, went out of her way to assist in apprehending criminals. The extra work we piled up was unbelievable. We owe her a debt of gratitude.

I went to the equal rank of Corporal; I never could figure that one out. I never wanted to be anything more than a Detective.

I spent five years in the Courts and the jail. I had been a Corporal in Communications when all of our male staff were replaced by females; I was one of the few who helped them and tried to train them. All I wanted was a good efficient police force. The women became very proficient, and I felt at times that they went out of their way to help me, as all I wanted to do was to catch crooks, rapists and child molesters and other types of scum.

And catch 'em I did!

Chain of Command ?

A Police Chief issued the following directive to his Superintendents:

"Tomorrow evening at approximately 2000 hours, Halley's Comet will be visible in this area, an event which occurs only once every seventy-five years. I will present a brief lecture on this rare phenomenon to all those who wish to assemble at the Police College training grounds. Those attending should be in the dress of the day. In case of rain, we will not be able to see anything, so assemble the men in the training centre auditorium and I will show them films of it."

Superintendents to District Inspectors:

"By order of the Chief Constable, tomorrow at 2000 hours, Haley's Comet will appear above the police college training area. If it rains, all those planning to attend will be marched to the auditorium where this rare phenomenon will take place, something which happens every seventy-five years."

District Inspectors to Squad Sergeants:

"By order of the Chief Constable at 2000 hours tomorrow evening the phenomenal Haley's Comet will appear in the police college auditorium. In case of rain in the auditorium, the Chief Constable will give another order, something which occurs once every seventy-five years."

Squad Sergeants to Squad Corporals:

"Tomorrow at 2000 hours, the Chief Constable will appear in the police college auditorium with Haley's Comet, something which happens every seventy years. If it rains, the Chief Constable will order the comet onto the college training grounds area."

Squad Corporals to Shift Constables:

"When it rains tomorrow at 2000 hours, the phenomenal seventy-five year old Chief Constable Hailey will drive his Comet through the police college auditorium."

...and so it goes...